Powerful Love
An Introduction to Christianity

Rev. Dr. Lloyd Strelow

Gospel Communication Resources

TRI-PILLAR PUBLISHING

POWERFUL LOVE

Copyright © 2010 by Lloyd Strelow

Tri-Pillar Publishing
Anaheim Hills, California
Website: www.TriPillarPublishing.com
e-mail: tripillarpublishing@cox.net

ALL RIGHTS RESERVED. This book or parts thereof may not be reproduced in any form without prior written permission of the publisher.

International Standard Book Number --13:   978-0-9818923-3-7

International Standard Book Number --10:   0-9818923-3-7

Library of Congress Catalog Card Number: 2010942359

Scripture taken from the HOLY BIBLE, NEW INTERNATIONAL VERSION©. NIV® Copyright© 1973, 1978, 1984, 2010 by International Bible Society. Used by permission of Zondervan. All rights reserved.

First edition, December, 2010

Printed in the United States of America

Dear Friend,

Thank you for accepting God's invitation to "Come and See" (John 1:46) what our Christian faith is all about.

We call this inductive study: ***Powerful Love***.

It has been said that love is a "many-splendored thing." Yet "love" is also widely misunderstood and greatly abused. It is absolutely true that many people look for love in all the wrong places.

The Good News is that God wants you to have genuine love – *His* love – at the center of your life!

Indeed, love is the very essence of our Christian faith and life! God's love touches every aspect of our daily living, and makes possible our eternal future with Him.

That we may know, have, and live God's ***Powerful Love*** in our lives is my prayer and the purpose of this study.

May the Holy Spirit richly bless your study of His Word!

Pastor Lloyd Strelow, D.Min.

Table of Contents

Powerful Love

Chapter	Page	Chapter Title	Theme
1	7	Love That Saves	"The Window" – Justification
		Now – as a Christian, I have:	
2	17	Love That Sustains	God the Father
3	25	Love That Redeems	God the Son
4	36	Love That Generates Faith	God the Holy Spirit
5	44	Love That Produces a New Birth	Baptism
6	52	Love That Strengthens	Holy Communion
7	60	Love That Gives Us Fellowship	The Church
8	71	Love That Tells It Like It Is	God's Word
9	79	Love That Directs Life – Toward God	1st Commandment
10	85	Love That Directs Life – Toward God	2nd & 3rd Commandments
11	96	Love That Directs Life – Toward Others	$4^{th} - 6^{th}$ Commandments
12	105	Love That Directs Life – Toward Others	$7^{th} - 10^{th}$ Commandments
13	112	Love That Lasts Forever	The End Times

Study Guidelines

Any book is only as helpful as it is understood and used. It is my prayer that these *Guidelines* will be a helpful tool in your personal inquiry into and study of God's **_POWERFUL LOVE_**.

1. This book is a "resource manual." A generous mixture of prayer, the Scriptures, the guidance of a capable teacher where possible, and many other resources – together with a searching student – are needed to be combined with this book for meaningful study and learning to take place. May God's Holy Spirit guide and bless your study!

2. In this study, the *NEW INTERNATIONAL VERSION (NIV)* – is used unless otherwise noted. In many places, passages are quoted at length to give you the context in which they are used in the Bible. You are encouraged to read entire passages directly from the Bible.

3. Words of Jesus in Scripture are printed in **bold, red** font.

4. The first chapter, regarding man's basic relationship with his Lord, is the most important lesson. It is also the "window" through which all other truths of God's Word must be seen!

5. Skills in Christian living – especially in worship, prayer, witnessing, and stewardship – are presented as part of the Christian life in the Ten Commandments.

6. If you are studying in a class, your questions and participation in discussion are heartily encouraged. If you are studying privately, ask your pastor for help and guidance.

7. Each lesson concludes with a special section that includes:
   a. A "worksheet" (referred to as "Food for Further Thought") designed to help you review, personalize, and apply God's Word to your own faith and life
   b. A Scripture reading guide of one chapter per day, which in 13 weeks will enable you to read:
   Mark, 1 John, Luke, Romans, 1 Corinthians, Ephesians, Philippians, and several Psalms
   c. A weekly Bible verse that you are encouraged to commit to memory

8. My goal is to use accurate, understandable language in this study. Where technical "theological" terms are needed and used, I have explained their meaning.

9. My goal is to share God's powerful love with you. In other words, I have not attempted to anticipate and answer every false teaching. Instead, I present what God says in His Word. It is the standard by which all teaching must be compared.

10. As you desire to grow in knowing and using God's powerful love in your life, regular worship is vitally important. In worship, God's people are renewed in faith and equipped for daily life – under the guidance of the Holy Spirit.

11. The greatest resource and asset is God's love richly and freely given in Christ and revealed in His Word!

Rev. Lloyd Strelow, D.Min. – Author & Pastor

Chapter 1

Love That Saves

Help! You have been called to the bedside of an old family friend, who has suffered a very serious heart attack. He confides in you that he is afraid to die. What will you say to him?

I. OUR NATURAL CONDITION
   A. *Where are we in life?*
      "The whole world is going 'mad'!" – Read the daily news.
      "**But** – I'm pretty good!"
   B. *How Good Are You?*
      1. By comparison with others?
      2. By comparison with God's standards?
         James 2:10 For whoever keeps the whole law and yet stumbles at just one point is guilty of breaking all of it.

SO GOD'S WORD TEACHES:
We are to live and evaluate our lives by God's will, rather than the world's standards. God demands total – 100% – obedience to Him and His will.

   C. *The Truth*
      1. How I am naturally:
         Psalm 51:5 Surely I was sinful at birth, sinful from the time my mother conceived me.
         Romans 5:12 Therefore, just as sin entered the world through one man, and death through sin, and in this way death came to all men, because all sinned –
         Genesis 5:3 When Adam had lived 130 years, he had a son in his own likeness, in his own image; and he named him Seth.
         Genesis 8:21 The LORD smelled the pleasing aroma and said in his heart: "Never again will I

curse the ground because of man, even though every inclination of his heart is evil from childhood. And never again will I destroy all living creatures, as I have done."

John 3:6 "Flesh gives birth to flesh, but the Spirit gives birth to spirit."

Romans 7:18 I know that nothing good lives in me, that is, in my sinful nature. For I have the desire to do what is good, but I cannot carry it out.

Romans 8:6-8 The mind of sinful man is death, but the mind controlled by the Spirit is life and peace; [7]the sinful mind is hostile to God. It does not submit to God's law, nor can it do so. [8]Those controlled by the sinful nature cannot please God.

SO GOD'S WORD TEACHES:

This "natural condition" that Scripture describes is called "original sin." This means that man is naturally separated from God, and by himself does not know, love, or serve God.

1. *What I do daily:*

    Matthew 15:19 "For out of the heart come evil thoughts, murder, adultery, sexual immorality, theft, false testimony, slander."

    Genesis 8:21 The LORD smelled the pleasing aroma and said in his heart: "Never again will I curse the ground because of man, even though every inclination of his heart is evil from childhood. And never again will I destroy all living creatures, as I have done."

    1 John 3:4 Everyone who sins breaks the law; in fact, sin is lawlessness.

James 4:17 Anyone, then, who knows the good he ought to do and doesn't do it, sins.

SO GOD'S WORD TEACHES:
Because we are naturally self-centered, we daily do what we desire. We often *fail to do* what God desires. We also often *actually do what God forbids*. All this is sin.

3. *Am I a sinner?*
   Romans 3:23 for all have sinned and fall short of the glory of God
   Romans 7:19 For what I do is not the good I want to do; no, the evil I do not want to do – this I keep on doing.
   Romans 3:10 As it is written: "There is no one righteous, not even one"
   Isaiah 64:6 All of us have become like one who is unclean, and all our righteous acts are like filthy rags; we all shrivel up like a leaf, and like the wind our sins sweep us away.
   1 John 1:8 If we claim to be without sin, we deceive ourselves and the truth is not in us.

SO GOD'S WORD TEACHES:
I am personally responsible to God, but have failed to live perfectly as He desires. I am a sinner who sins daily. I need to examine my life this past week in the light of the Ten Commandments.

D. *The Proper Result*
   1. *Spiritual Death*
      Isaiah 59:2 But your iniquities have separated you from your God; your sins have hidden his face from you, so that he will not hear.

2. *Temporal or physical death*
   Romans 5:12 Therefore, just as sin entered the world through one man, and death through sin, and in this way death came to all men, because all sinned –
3. *Eternal death*
   Romans 6:23 For the wages of sin is death, but the gift of God is eternal life in Christ Jesus our Lord.

SO GOD'S WORD TEACHES:

Sin pulls the sinner (us) away from God. The result of sin is God's just and holy anger. It is the nature of a holy God that he cannot tolerate sin; He must punish it. The sinner deserves separation from God.

E. *Let's Make Up With God!*
   Luke 17:10 "So you also, when you have done everything you were told to do, should say, 'We are unworthy servants; we have only done our duty.'"
   Romans 3:28 For we maintain that a man is justified by faith apart from observing the law.
   Ephes. 2:8-9 For it is by grace you have been saved, through faith – and this not from yourselves, it is the gift of God – ^{9}not by works, so that no one can boast.

SO GOD'S WORD TEACHES:

Whatever good we do is only what God rightfully expects. It can never atone or make up for our past sins. Peace with God can never be earned by me or gained by my attempts to keep God's law.

II A NEW LIFE
A. *God's Desire For Us*

2 Peter 3:9 The Lord is not slow in keeping his promise, as some understand slowness. He is patient with you, not wanting anyone to perish, but everyone to come to repentance.

SO GOD'S WORD TEACHES:

God has no joy in punishing sinners. Instead, He wants them to have a joyful, peace-filled, purposeful life now and forever.

B. *There Is A Way*
1. *Our Substitute*

2 Cor. 5:21 God made him who had no sin to be sin for us, so that in him we might become the righteousness of God.

1 John 2:2 He is the atoning sacrifice for our sins, and not only for ours but also for the sins of the whole world.

1 Peter 2:24 He himself bore our sins in his body on the tree, so that we might die to sins and live for righteousness; by his wounds you have been healed.

Isaiah 53:5-6 But he was pierced for our transgressions, he was crushed for our iniquities; the punishment that brought us peace was upon him, and by his wounds we are healed. ⁶We all, like sheep, have gone astray, each of us has turned to his own way; and the LORD has laid on him the iniquity of us all.

2. *To Satisfy God's Justice*

Romans 4:23-25 The words "it was credited to him" were written not for him alone, ²⁴but also for us, to whom God will credit righteousness – for us who believe in him who raised Jesus our Lord from the dead. [25]He was delivered over to death for our sins and was raised to life for our justification.

1 John 4:10 This is love: not that we loved God, but that he loved us and sent his Son as an atoning sacrifice for our sins.

3. *The Only Way*

    Acts 4:10 "then know this, you and all the people of Israel: It is by the name of Jesus Christ of Nazareth, whom you crucified but whom God raised from the dead, that this man stands before you healed."

    Acts 4:12 "Salvation is found in no one else, for there is no other name under heaven given to men by which we must be saved."

SO GOD'S WORD TEACHES:

Because He loves us, Jesus rescued us from guilt, the power of sin, and eternal separation from God. He did this by paying the penalty of our sin for us on the cross of Calvary. He is the only way to peace with God.

C. *God Says:*

   Romans 8:1 Therefore, there is now no condemnation for those who are in Christ Jesus,

   Romans 3:23-24 for all have sinned and fall short of the glory of God, [24]and are justified freely by his grace through the redemption that came by Christ Jesus.

   Romans 4:5 However, to the man who does not work but trusts God who justifies the wicked, his faith is credited as righteousness.

SO GOD'S WORD TEACHES:
Though we are sinners, God declares us "**NOT GUILTY**" because Jesus already paid our debt.

D. *Faith*

Acts 16:31 They replied, "Believe in the Lord Jesus, and you will be saved – you and your household."

James 2:19 You believe that there is one God. Good! Even the demons believe that – and shudder.

Romans 4:3 What does the Scripture say? "Abraham believed God, and it was credited to him as righteousness."

Romans 3:22 This righteousness from God comes through faith in Jesus Christ to all who believe. There is no difference,

Romans 3:28 For we maintain that a man is justified by faith apart from observing the law.

Romans 4:5 However, to the man who does not work but trusts God who justifies the wicked, his faith is credited as righteousness.

SO GOD'S WORD TEACHES:
We accept God's love and pardon by faith. Faith includes much more than merely knowing that there is a God, and agreeing that God and His Word are true. Faith is accepting His love, and trusting Him to forgive me fully, bring me into His family, and love me richly and daily.

E. *Can I Be Sure?*

Titus 2:1-2 You must teach what is in accord with sound doctrine. ²Teach the older men to be temperate, worthy of respect, self-controlled, and sound in faith, in love and in endurance.

Romans 8:38-39 For I am convinced that neither death nor life, neither angels nor demons, neither the present nor the future, nor any powers, ^{39}neither height nor depth, nor anything else in all creation, will be able to separate us from the love of God that is in Christ Jesus our Lord.

Phil. 1:6 being confident of this, that he who began a good work in you will carry it on to completion until the day of Christ Jesus.

SO GOD'S WORD TEACHES:

We can be absolutely sure of forgiveness, life, salvation, and heaven itself! Our certainty is not based on our reason or feelings, but on God's changeless, rich love and promises.

SUMMARY

This is the most important truth you will ever study! *In His great love, God comes and gives you: light for darkness, love for anger, Christ for you, forgiveness for your sin, and life for death! May this powerful love of God fill you and dwell in you richly*!

FOOD FOR FURTHER THOUGHT

1. Why is "guilt" such a problem with people?

2. "Sin brings death." – Explain

3. Can God be – at the same time – both a loving God and a just God who punishes sin? Discuss your answer.

4. Why is Jesus' death and resurrection so important for Christians today?

5. Susan has read her Bible and agrees that Jesus lived and died on the cross. Is this enough to get her to heaven? Explain.

6. Define "grace."

7. What would you tell Karen who complains: "I know Jesus died for me, but I just don't feel like I'm saved?"

8. Write **Yes or No** for each statement as it applies to you personally.

　　　　　 a I believe I am a sinner who has done what God forbids, and failed to do what He requires.

　　　　　 b I believe that I naturally deserve to go to hell.

　　　　　 c I believe I cannot save myself from God's anger.

　　　　　 d I believe that Jesus – as my Substitute – died for my sin and rose to give me forgiveness and a new life.

　　　　　 e I am sure that when I die, I will go to heaven.

　　　　　 f My certainty of heaven depends on Jesus, not on me.

9. Write **your name** in each blank, and then read the passage out loud:

For God so loved _____ that He gave His one and only Son, that if _____ believes in Him, _____ shall not perish, but _____ will have eternal life.

– ***John 3:16*** *paraphrased* (Often called **"The Gospel in a nutshell"**)

DAILY GROWTH TROUGH BIBLE READING

1st Day – Mark 1
2nd Day – Mark 2
3rd Day – Mark 3
4th Day – Mark 4
5th Day – Mark 5
6th Day – Mark 6
7th Day – Mark 7

A SCRIPTURAL GEM – For the Memory:

Ephesians 2:8-9
For it is by grace you have been saved,
through faith –
and this not from yourselves,
it is the gift of God –
^{9}not by works,
so that no one can boast.

Chapter 2

Love That Sustains – God the Father

Too often we hear the sad story of another baby found abandoned at a church, supermarket, or hospital. Thank God that He does not just have a love that saves us; He also gives us His love that sustains us.

I. **GOD'S QUALITIES - Identify from the Bible verse:**

_____ **John 4:24** "God is spirit, and his worshipers must worship in spirit and in truth."

_____ **1 John 4:8** Whoever does not love does not know God, because God is love.

_____ **Leviticus 19:2** Speak to the entire assembly of Israel and say to them: "Be holy because I, the LORD your God, am holy."

_____ **Psalm 90:2** Before the mountains were born or you brought forth the earth and the world, from everlasting to everlasting you are God.

_____ **Malachi 3:6** "I the LORD do not change. So you, O descendants of Jacob, are not destroyed."

_____ **Genesis 17:1** When Abram was ninety-nine years old, the Lord appeared to him and said, "I am God Almighty; walk before me and be blameless."

_____ **1 John 3:19-20** This then is how we know that we belong to the truth, and how we set our hearts at rest in his presence [20]whenever our hearts condemn us. For God is greater than our hearts, and he knows everything.

_____ **Jeremiah 23:24** "Can anyone hide in secret places so that I cannot see him?" declares the LORD. "Do not I fill heaven and earth?" declares the LORD.

_____ **Deut. 32:4** He is the Rock, his works are perfect, and all his ways are just. A faithful God who does no wrong, upright and just is he.

_____ **2 Tim. 2:13** if we are faithless, he will remain faithful, for he cannot disown himself.

SO GOD'S WORD TEACHES:

Our God has many magnificent qualities, which He alone possesses.

II THE ONLY GOD

Deut. 6:4 Hear, O Israel: The LORD our God, the LORD is one.

Matthew 28:19 **"Therefore go and make disciples of all nations, baptizing them in the name of the Father and of the Son and of the Holy Spirit."**

SO GOD'S WORD TEACHES:

There is only one God; but there are three persons in the God-head. The one true God is the Triune God. God does not expect us to fully understand Him, but to accept Him as He really is and reveals Himself to us.

III THE FATHER
A. *Creation*
1. The World

Hebrews 3:4 For every house is built by someone, but God is the builder of everything.

Genesis 1:1 In the beginning God created the heavens and the earth.

Exodus 20:11 For in six days the LORD made the heavens and the earth, the sea, and all that is in them, but he rested on the seventh day. Therefore the LORD blessed the Sabbath day and made it holy.

Hebrews 11:3 By faith we understand that the universe was formed at God's command, so that what is seen was not made out of what was visible.

Genesis 1:31 God saw all that he had made, and it was very good. And there was evening, and there was morning – the sixth day.

SO GOD'S WORD TEACHES:

By His almighty Word, God made our wonderful world, with all of its "natural resources," out of nothing. He created a beautiful and perfect world for us.

2. Angels

Hebrews 1:14 Are not all angels ministering spirits sent to serve those who will inherit salvation?

Luke 2:13 Suddenly a great company of the heavenly host appeared with the angel, praising God …

Psalm 103:20 Praise the LORD, you his angels, you mighty ones who do his bidding, who obey his word.

2 Peter 2:4 For if God did not spare angels when they sinned, but sent them to hell, putting them into gloomy dungeons to be held for judgment …

John 8:44 *"You belong to your father, the devil, and you want to carry out your father's desire. He was a murderer from the beginning, not holding to the truth, for there is no truth in him. When he lies, he speaks his native language, for he is a liar and the father of lies."*

Mark 5:9 Then Jesus asked him, *"What is your name?"* "My name is Legion," he replied, "for we are many."

1 Peter 5:8 Be self-controlled and alert. Your enemy the devil prowls around like a roaring lion looking for someone to devour.

SO GOD'S WORD TEACHES:

There are many angels – both good and evil. Both types are powerful. The good angels gladly serve God. The fallen angels (including Satan, the devil) fight against God and His children.

   3. *People*

   Genesis 2:7 the LORD God formed the man from the dust of the ground and breathed into his nostrils the breath of life, and the man became a living being.

   Genesis 1:27 So God created man in his own image, in the image of God he created him; male and female he created them.

   Col. 3:10 (You) … have put on the new self, which is being renewed in knowledge in the image of its Creator.

Ephesians 4:22 & 24 … put off your old self …
²⁴and to put on the new self, created to be like God in true righteousness and holiness.

SO GOD'S WORD TEACHES:

God not only created man by a special act, but he made man like God – holy, righteous, blessed with all he needed. Man was to be in charge of all of God's creation.

B. *Daily Care*

Psalm 36:6 Your righteousness is like the mighty mountains, your justice like the great deep. O LORD, you preserve both man and beast.

Psalm 145:15-16 The eyes of all look to you, and you give them their food at the proper time. ¹⁶You open your hand and satisfy the desires of every living thing.

Matthew 10:29-31 "Are not two sparrows sold for a penny? Yet not one of them will fall to the ground apart from the will of your Father. ³⁰And even the very hairs of your head are all numbered. ³¹So don't be afraid; you are worth more than many sparrows."

Romans 8:32 He who did not spare his own Son, but gave him up for us all – how will he not also, along with him, graciously give us all things?

Psalm 139:14 I praise you because I am fearfully and wonderfully made; your works are wonderful, I know that full well.

Hebrews 1:3 The Son is the radiance of God's glory and the exact representation of his being, sustaining all things by his powerful word. After he had provided purification for sins, he sat down at the right hand of the Majesty in heaven.

Romans 8:35-39 Who shall separate us from the love of Christ? Shall trouble or hardship or persecution or famine or nakedness or danger or sword? [36]As it is written: "For your sake we face death all day long; we are considered as sheep to be slaughtered." [37]No, in all these things we are more than conquerors through him who loved us. [38]For I am convinced that neither death nor life, neither angels nor demons, neither the present nor the future, nor any powers, [39]neither height nor depth, nor anything else in all creation, will be able to separate us from the love of God that is in Christ Jesus our Lord.

Romans 8:28 And we know that in all things God works for the good of those who love him, who have been called according to his purpose.

Genesis 50:20 You intended to harm me, but God intended it for good to accomplish what is now being done, the saving of many lives.

Hebrews 12:5-8 And you have forgotten that word of encouragement that addresses you as sons: "My son, do not make light of the Lord's discipline, and do not lose heart when he rebukes you, [6]because the Lord disciplines those he loves, and he punishes everyone he accepts as a son." [7]Endure hardship as discipline; God is treating you as sons. For what son is not disciplined by his father? [8]If you are not disciplined (and everyone undergoes discipline), then you are illegitimate children and not true sons.

SO GOD'S WORD TEACHES:

By His great power, according to His wisdom, and out of His love for us in every need every day, God daily provides for us. He is able to turn apparent disaster into a blessing. He sometimes corrects us and draws us closer to Himself. His love will never leave His children!

Love That Sustains – God the Father

C. *Our Response*

Genesis 32:10 I am unworthy of all the kindness and faithfulness you have shown your servant. I had only my staff when I crossed this Jordan, but now I have become two groups.

Psalm 116:12 How can I repay the LORD for all his goodness to me?

Psalm 118:1 Give thanks to the LORD, for he is good; his love endures forever.

Psalm 31:14-15 But I trust in you, O LORD; I say, "You are my God." [15]My times are in your hands; deliver me from my enemies and from those who pursue me.

Psalm 37:5 Commit your way to the LORD; trust in him and he will do this:

1 Peter 5:7 Cast all your anxiety on him because he cares for you.

SO GOD'S WORD TEACHES:

Humility, thankfulness, and trust should be our response to God's loving daily care and blessings. God is merciful. We should be grateful and responsible in our use of His gifts. As those who know they have a loving Heavenly Father, we should depend on Him to fill our every need.

FOOD FOR FURTHER THOUGHT

1. Carl is not a Christian, yet he believes God is all-knowing and all-powerful. How will Carl probably feel?

2. God is unchanging. How does this truth comfort you as a Christian?

3. Can you "prove" the Trinity? – Explain

4. Why is evolution wrong?

5. What relationship does Thanksgiving have to this lesson – and The First Article?

6. "Christians should make the best caretakers of the environment?" – Agree or disagree? – Why?

7. Jesus taught us to pray: "Give us this day our dally bread." Name at least five things meant by "daily bread."

8. Why is worry a sin?

9. How can Christians conquer worry?

DAILY GROWTH TROUGH BIBLE READING

1st Day – Mark 8
2nd Day – Mark 9
3rd Day – Mark 10
4th Day – Mark 11
5th Day – Mark 12
6th Day – Mark 13
7th Day – Mark 14

A SCRIPTURAL GEM – For the Memory:

Romans 8:28
And we know that in all things
   God works
      for the good of those who love him,
         who have been called according to his purpose.

Chapter 3

Love That Redeems – God the Son

Surely Jesus of Nazareth is the most controversial person in all of human history! He is also the most important, due both to His role in history and to His powerful love for me. It is vitally important that we know just who Jesus really is!

I. **COMMON IDEAS OF WHO JESUS IS:**
Good man and noble example ~ Moral teacher ~ Miracle worker ~ Rebel ~ Martyr

YET GOD'S WORD TEACHES:
There is some truth in all of these titles. Yet to really "know" Jesus, you must look much deeper. Read on!

II. **WHO IS HE?**
   A. **True God – Divine Nature**

     Romans 9:5 Theirs are the patriarchs, and from them is traced the human ancestry of Christ, who is God over all, forever praised! Amen.

     Matthew 16:13,15,16 When Jesus came to the region of Caesarea Philippi, he asked his disciples, **"Who do people say the Son of Man is?"** … [15]**"But what about you?"** **he asked.** **"Who do you say I am?"** [16]Simon Peter answered, "You are the Christ, the Son of the living God."

     1 John 5:20 We know also that the Son of God has come and has given us understanding, so that we may know him who is true. And we are in him who is true

– even in his Son Jesus Christ. He is the true God and eternal life.

John 1:1 In the beginning was the Word, and the Word was with God, and the Word was God.

Hebrews 13:8 Jesus Christ is the same yesterday and today and forever.

Matthew 28:20 "... **and teaching them to obey everything I have commanded you. And surely I am with you always, to the very end of the age.**"

John 21:17 The third time he said to him, "**Simon son of John, do you love me?**" Peter was hurt because Jesus asked him the third time, "**Do you love me?**" He said, "Lord, you know all things; you know that I love you." Jesus said, "**Feed my sheep.**"

Matthew 28:18 Then Jesus came to them and said, "**All authority in heaven and on earth has been given to me.**"

John 1:3 Through him all things were made; without him nothing was made that has been made.

Hebrews 1:3 The Son is the radiance of God's glory and the exact representation of his being, sustaining all things by his powerful word. After he had provided purification for sins, he sat down at the right hand of the Majesty in heaven.

Matthew 9:6 "**But so that you may know that the Son of Man has authority on earth to forgive sins....**" Then he said to the paralytic, "**Get up, take your mat and go home.**"

SO GOD'S WORD TEACHES:

There is no doubt about it; the Scriptures call Jesus "God." He is divine! Furthermore, Jesus has all the ability of God and does things only God can do. He has the glory of God. The claim that Jesus is not really God is one of the earliest heresies (false teachings).

B. True Man - Human Nature

1 Tim. 2:5 For there is one God and one mediator between God and men, the man Christ Jesus,

John 1:14 The Word became flesh and made his dwelling among us. We have seen his glory, the glory of the One and Only, who came from the Father, full of grace and truth.

John 11:35 Jesus wept.

Hebrews 4:15 For we do not have a high priest who is unable to sympathize with our weaknesses, but we have one who has been tempted in every way, just as we are – yet was without sin.

SO GOD'S WORD TEACHES:

Jesus was a real human being with feelings, emotions, and actions that all people have. He slept, ate, and rested like other people. Jesus was different from other people in one important way: He never sinned.

C. The Importance of Jesus Being Both God and Man

Psalm 49:7 No man can redeem the life of another or give to God a ransom for him –

Hebrews 2:14 Since the children have flesh and blood, he too shared in their humanity so that by his death he might destroy him who holds the power of death – that is, the devil –

SO GOD'S WORD TEACHES:

Jesus has a human nature in order to be our real Substitute and pay the price of sin in our place. His divine nature assures us that He did not do this for Himself, but that His life, death, and resurrection are sufficient for our victory over sin, death, and hell.

III. JESUS' LIFE ON EARTH
A. A Miraculous Conception

Luke 1:35 The angel answered, "The Holy Spirit will come upon you, and the power of the Most High will overshadow you. So the holy one to be born will be called the Son of God."

Matthew 1:20 But after he had considered this, an angel of the Lord appeared to him in a dream and said, "Joseph son of David, do not be afraid to take Mary home as your wife, because what is conceived in her is from the Holy Spirit."

B. Birth In Bethlehem

Isaiah 7:14 Therefore the Lord himself will give you a sign: The virgin will be with child and will give birth to a son, and will call him Immanuel.

Luke 2:7 and she gave birth to her firstborn, a son. She wrapped him in cloths and placed him in a manger, because there was no room for them in the inn.

John 1:14 The Word became flesh and made his dwelling among us. We have seen his glory, the glory of the One and Only, who came from the Father, full of grace and truth.

C. His Life

Luke 2:52 And Jesus grew in wisdom and stature, and in favor with God and men.

Galatians 4:4-5 But when the time had fully come, God sent his Son, born of a woman, born under law, ^{5}to redeem those under law, that we might receive the full rights of sons.

Romans 5:19 For just as through the disobedience of the one man the many were made sinners, so also through the obedience of the one man the many will be made righteous.

SO GOD'S WORD TEACHES:
Jesus left His throne in heaven and became our "brother." He grew up into young manhood. When He was about 30 years old, He began His public ministry of preaching God's kingdom and sharing His love. He played no favorites. He minced no words. He exposed sin, then offered God's healing love and power. He usually did not use His divine power; His miracles are an exception to show He is truly the mighty Son of God.

IV. JESUS' DEATH
A. Jesus – Captured, Condemned, and Crucified
Galatians 3:13 Christ redeemed us from the curse of the law by becoming a curse for us, for it is written: "Cursed is everyone who is hung on a tree."

John 19:30 When he had received the drink, Jesus said, **"It is finished."** With that, he bowed his head and gave up his spirit.

B. He Is Holy, Without Sin
1 Peter 1:18-19 For you know that it was not with perishable things such as silver or gold that you were redeemed from the empty way of life handed down to you from your forefathers, [19]but with the precious blood of Christ, a lamb without blemish or defect.

C. A Complete Triumph – Of Love, To Save Us
Matthew 1:21 "She will give birth to a son, and you are to give him the name Jesus, because he will save his people from their sins."

2 Cor. 5:21 God made him who had no sin to be sin for us, so that in him we might become the righteousness of God.
Isaiah 53:5 But he was pierced for our transgressions, he was crushed for our iniquities; the punishment that brought us peace was upon him, and by his wounds we are healed.
1 Cor. 15:3 For what I received I passed on to you as of first importance: that Christ died for our sins according to the Scriptures

D. Love For All
2 Cor. 5:15 And he died for all, that those who live should no longer live for themselves but for him who died for them and was raised again.
1 John 2:2 He is the atoning sacrifice for our sins, and not only for ours but also for the sins of the whole world.

SO GOD'S WORD TEACHES:
Many good and noble people have died and were soon forgotten. With Jesus, the "impossible" happened! The Son of God gave His life willingly for me. He was cursed that I might be blessed. He absorbed God's righteous anger that I might know only love. He died so that I could live!

V. JESUS ROSE FROM THE DEAD!
A. It Is a Fact
Luke 24:5-7 In their fright the women bowed down with their faces to the ground, but the men said to them, "Why do you look for the living among the dead? ⁶He is not here; he has risen! Remember how he told you, while he was still with you in Galilee: ⁷'The Son of Man must be delivered into the hands of sinful

men, be crucified and on the third day be raised again.'"

Acts 2:24 But God raised him from the dead, freeing him from the agony of death, because it was impossible for death to keep its hold on him.

Rev. 1:18 "I am the Living One; I was dead, and behold I am alive for ever and ever! And I hold the keys of death and Hades."

B. **The Evidence**
   1. Jesus descended into hell – neither to suffer nor to convert people – but to proclaim His victory in the midst of the enemy's camp.

      1 Peter 3:18 For Christ died for sins once for all, the righteous for the unrighteous, to bring you to God. He was put to death in the body but made alive by the Spirit

   2. In the 40 days following His resurrection, Jesus frequently appeared to His disciples.

      Acts 1:3 After his suffering, he showed himself to these men and gave many convincing proofs that he was alive. He appeared to them over a period of forty days and spoke about the kingdom of God.

      1 Cor. 15:3-8 For what I received I passed on to you as of first importance: that Christ died for our sins according to the Scriptures, [4]that he was buried, that he was raised on the third day according to the Scriptures, [5]and that he appeared to Peter, and then to the Twelve. [6]After that, he appeared to more than five hundred of the brothers at the same time, most of whom are still living, though some have fallen asleep. [7]Then he appeared to James, then to all the apostles, [8]and

last of all he appeared to me also, as to one abnormally born.

C. **The Blessing**
   1. **We know He is the Mighty God.**
      Romans 1:4 and who through the Spirit of holiness was declared with power to be the Son of God by his resurrection from the dead: Jesus Christ our Lord.

   2. **We can trust His Word.**
      John 2:19-21 Jesus answered them, **"Destroy this temple, and I will raise it again in three days."** [20]The Jews replied, "It has taken forty-six years to build this temple, and you are going to raise it in three days?" [21]But the temple he had spoken of was his body.
      Matthew 28:6 "He is not here; he has risen, just as he said. Come and see the place where he lay."
      1 Cor. 15:17 And if Christ has not been raised, your faith is futile; you are still in your sins.

   3. **We are assured of life in heaven with Jesus**.
      1 Cor. 15:20-23 But Christ has indeed been raised from the dead, the first fruits of those who have fallen asleep. [21]For since death came through a man, the resurrection of the dead comes also through a man. [22]For as in Adam all die, so in Christ all will be made alive. [23]But each in his own turn: Christ, the first fruits; then, when he comes, those who belong to him.

SO GOD'S WORD TEACHES:
The resurrection of Jesus from the dead is a fact. He kept His promise. We are free from sin's punishment. The

Father accepted His Son's sacrifice. He conquered man's last enemy. His resurrection assures us of our resurrection to life with Him forever. What a Savior! Good Friday and Easter go together. He died for us, but lives again. No wonder the Christian Church has chosen Sunday – the day of Christ's resurrection – as its regular day of worship!

VI. JESUS' ASCENSION

Acts 1:9 After he said this, he was taken up before their very eyes, and a cloud hid him from their sight.

Matthew 28:18-20 Then Jesus came to them and said, **"All authority in heaven and on earth has been given to me. [19]Therefore go and make disciples of all nations, baptizing them in the name of the Father and of the Son and of the Holy Spirit, [20]and teaching them to obey everything I have commanded you. And surely I am with you always, to the very end of the age."**

SO GOD'S WORD TEACHES:

Jesus spent 40 days after His resurrection appearing to His disciples and giving them their great task in life – to share God's powerful love in Him. Then He ascended – bodily – into heaven.

VII. JESUS RULES – "Sits at the right hand of God"

Eph. 1:19-22 That power is like the working of his mighty strength, [20]which he exerted in Christ when he raised him from the dead and seated him at his right hand in the heavenly realms, [21]far above all rule and authority, power and dominion, and every title that can be given, not only in the present age but also in the one to come. [22]And God placed all things under his feet and appointed him to be head over everything for the church

Romans 8:34 Who is he that condemns? Christ Jesus, who died – more than that, who was raised to life – is at the right hand of God and is also interceding for us.

John 14:3 "And if I go and prepare a place for you, I will come back and take you to be with me that you also may be where I am."

SO GOD'S WORD TEACHES:
Jesus is the exalted Lord. He uses His divine power to care for the world, especially for His body, the Church.

JESUS: A *mere* teacher, example, rebel, miracle, worker, martyr?

JESUS: **A *thousand times more* – my Savior, Lord, and Friend!**

FOOD FOR FURTHER THOUGHT

1. What role did Mary play in Jesus' life?

2. What role did Mary have in our salvation?

3. How should Christians honor Mary?

4. Explain how Jesus' miracles were different from those of Moses or Peter.

5. Why is the fact of Jesus' death and resurrection so important to you?

6. In the Apostles' Creed, we say we believe that Jesus "descended into hell." How does the *way we say that* perhaps show *what we believe* regarding that visit?

7. You have a friend who says: "Jesus was born like any

other person, and then he died a martyr's death." What would you say to your friend?

8. If Jesus had been only a human being, what difference would it make for your faith and salvation?

9. Which is more important: Jesus' death or His resurrection?

10. Why did Jesus perform miracles?

DAILY GROWTH TROUGH BIBLE READING

1st Day – Mark 15
2nd Day – Mark 16
3rd Day – 1 John 1
4th Day – 1 John 2
5th Day – 1 John 3
6th Day – 1 John 4
7th Day – 1 John 5

A SCRIPTURAL GEM – For the Memory:

1 John 4:10
This is love:
 not that we loved God,
 but that he loved us
 and sent his Son
  as an atoning sacrifice
  for our sins.

Chapter 4

Love That Generates Faith – God the Holy Spirit

Childhood memories of "ghosts and goblins" is about the only connection many people have with any "spirit." What a far cry goblins are from God's love in pouring out His Holy Spirit!

I. **WHO IS THE HOLY SPIRIT?**
Matthew 28:19 "Therefore go and make disciples of all nations, baptizing them in the name of the Father and of the Son and of the Holy Spirit"
Acts 5:3-4 Then Peter said, "Ananias, how is it that Satan has so filled your heart that you have lied to the Holy Spirit and have kept for yourself some of the money you received for the land? ⁴Didn't it belong to you before it was sold? And after it was sold, wasn't the money at your disposal? What made you think of doing such a thing? You have not lied to men but to God."

SO GOD'S WORD TEACHES:
The Holy Spirit is God, part of the Trinity. He is also called the "Comforter" and the "Holy Ghost."

II. **THE OUTPOURING OF THE HOLY SPIRIT**
Acts 2:1 & 4 When the day of Pentecost came, they were all together in one place. ... ⁴All of them were filled with the Holy Spirit and began to speak in other tongues as the Spirit enabled them.

Love That Generates Faith – God the Holy Spirit

SO GOD'S WORD TEACHES:
Ten days after Jesus' ascension, the Holy Spirit was poured out on the disciples. Under the Spirit's blessing, Peter preached the Gospel with power, and about 3,000 people became Christians that day.

III. THE MAIN WORK OF THE HOLY SPIRIT

John 14:6 Jesus answered, **"I am the way and the truth and the life. No one comes to the Father except through me."**

Acts 16:31 They replied, "Believe in the Lord Jesus, and you will be saved – you and your household."

1 Cor. 12:3 Therefore I tell you that no one who is speaking by the Spirit of God says, "Jesus be cursed," and no one can say, "Jesus is Lord," except by the Holy Spirit.

Eph. 2:1 As for you, you were dead in your transgressions and sins

Romans 8:7 the sinful mind is hostile to God. It does not submit to God's law, nor can it do so.

1 Cor. 2:14 The man without the Spirit does not accept the things that come from the Spirit of God, for they are foolishness to him, and he cannot understand them, because they are spiritually discerned.

SO GOD'S WORD TEACHES:
Faith in Jesus as one's personal Savior is absolutely necessary for salvation. However, man is naturally incapable – by himself – of coming to faith in Jesus. The main work of the Holy Spirit is to give us that saving faith in Jesus.

IV. THE HOLY SPIRIT'S METHOD

Romans 10:17 Consequently, faith comes from hearing the message, and the message is heard through the word of Christ.

2 Thes. 2:14 He called you to this through our gospel, that you might share in the glory of our Lord Jesus Christ.

1 Peter 1:23 For you have been born again, not of perishable seed, but of imperishable, through the living and enduring word of God.

Romans 1:16 I am not ashamed of the gospel, because it is the power of God for the salvation of everyone who believes: first for the Jew, then for the Gentile.

Acts 2:41 Those who accepted his message were baptized, and about three thousand were added to their number that day.

SO GOD'S WORD TEACHES:

The Holy Spirit has chosen to give and sustain faith through the channel (means) of the Word (Bible) and the Sacraments. We call these the *"means of grace."* It is God's Word that has the power to lead people to accept Jesus as Savior.

V. A NEW BEGINNING

Eph. 5:8 For you were once darkness, but now you are light in the Lord. Live as children of light

Eph. 2:4-5 But because of his great love for us, God, who is rich in mercy, ⁵made us alive with Christ even when we were dead in transgressions – it is by grace you have been saved.

1 Peter 1:23 For you have been born again, not of perishable seed, but of imperishable, through the living and enduring word of God.

1 Peter 2:25 For you were like sheep going astray, but now you have returned to the Shepherd and Overseer of your souls.

SO GOD'S WORD TEACHES:
Regeneration, conversion, new-birth – these are various ways of describing the beginning of our new life by faith in Jesus Christ.

VI. PERSONALLY

Acts 16:29-31 The jailer called for lights, rushed in and fell trembling before Paul and Silas. ³⁰He then brought them out and asked, "Sirs, what must I do to be saved?" ³¹They replied, "Believe in the Lord Jesus, and you will be saved – you and your household."

Hebrews 4:7 Therefore God again set a certain day, calling it Today, when a long time later he spoke through David, as was said before: "Today, if you hear his voice, do not harden your hearts."

Mark 1:15 **"The time has come,"** he said**. "The kingdom of God is near. Repent and believe the good news!"**

SO GOD'S WORD TEACHES:
Working through the Word, the Holy Spirit leads me to repent of my sin and fills my heart with my very own personal faith in Christ my Savior.

VII. A NEW LIFE!

2 Cor. 5:17 Therefore, if anyone is in Christ, he is a new creation; the old has gone, the new has come!

Eph. 2:10 For we are God's workmanship, created in Christ Jesus to do good works, which God prepared in advance for us to do.

Romans 8:16 The Spirit himself testifies with our spirit that we are God's children.

Romans 8:26 In the same way, the Spirit helps us in our weakness. We do not know what we ought to pray for, but the Spirit himself intercedes for us with groans that words cannot express.

1 Cor. 10:13 No temptation has seized you except what is common to man. And God is faithful; he will not let you be tempted beyond what you can bear. But when you are tempted, he will also provide a way out so that you can stand up under it.

1 Thes. 2:13 And we also thank God continually because, when you received the word of God, which you heard from us, you accepted it not as the word of men, but as it actually is, the word of God, which is at work in you who believe.

Phil. 2:13 for it is God who works in you to will and to act according to his good purpose.

SO GOD'S WORD TEACHES:

The Holy Spirit nourishes, guides, and protects us so that daily our faith will grow stronger and our lives more Christ-like. He does this primarily through the Word and Sacrament – the "means of grace."

VIII. TO HEAVEN

1 Peter 1:5 … you, ⁵who through faith are shielded by God's power until the coming of the salvation that is ready to be revealed in the last time.

Phil. 1:6 being confident of this, that he who began a good work in you will carry it on to completion until the day of Christ Jesus.

SO GOD'S WORD TEACHES:

Christians rejoice because they trust the sure promise of the Holy Spirit to keep their faith strong until they meet Jesus in heaven.

Love That Generates Faith – God the Holy Spirit 41

IX. A BIG QUESTION: *Why are some people Christians and other people unbelievers?*

1 Tim. 2:3-4 This is good, and pleases God our Savior, ⁴who wants all men to be saved and to come to a knowledge of the truth.

Ezekiel 33:11 Say to them, "As surely as I live, declares the Sovereign LORD, I take no pleasure in the death of the wicked, but rather that they turn from their ways and live. Turn! Turn from your evil ways! Why will you die, O house of Israel?"

2 Peter 3:9 The Lord is not slow in keeping his promise, as some understand slowness. He is patient with you, not wanting anyone to perish, but everyone to come to repentance.

Matthew 23:37 "O Jerusalem, Jerusalem, you who kill the prophets and stone those sent to you, how often I have longed to gather your children together, as a hen gathers her chicks under her wings, but you were not willing."

Acts 7:51 "You stiff-necked people, with uncircumcised hearts and ears! You are just like your fathers: You always resist the Holy Spirit!"

Mark 16:16 "Whoever believes and is baptized will be saved, but whoever does not believe will be condemned."

SO GOD'S WORD TEACHES:

Just as Jesus died for all people, so our Lord sincerely wants all to repent and believe. He never arbitrarily loves some and rejects others! If we are without God's love in Christ, the fault is always our lack of faith due to our rejection of the Holy Spirit.

FOOD FOR FURTHER THOUGHT

1. Can a person be a "half-Christian?" – Explain your answer.

2. Your best friend tells you that he/she "made a decision for Christ." What will be your response?

3. Why is a "self-produced" Christian an impossibility?

4. Where do you get faith?

5. Remembering the work of the Holy Spirit, what value is Bible study?

6. Are you sure your sins are forgiven and you are going to heaven? Why?

7. Check the appropriate response for the following:
   A ___ Agree ___ Disagree – Every Christian must be "baptized in the Holy Spirit."
   B ___ Agree ___ Disagree – You are not a Christian unless you've had an "emotional experience" with the Lord.
   C ___ Agree ___ Disagree – If you "speak in tongues," you are a better Christian than if you don't speak that way.

   WHY did you respond that way?

Love That Generates Faith – God the Holy Spirit

DAILY GROWTH TROUGH BIBLE READING

1st Day – Luke 1
2nd Day – Luke 2
3rd Day – Luke 3
4th Day – Luke 4
5th Day – Luke 5
6th Day – Luke 6
7th Day – Luke 7

A SCRIPTURAL GEM – For the Memory:

1 Corinthians 10:13

No temptation has seized you except what is common to man.
And God is faithful;
he will not let you be tempted beyond what you can bear.
But when you are tempted,
he will also provide a way out so that you can stand up under it.

Chapter 5

Love That Produces a New Birth – Holy Baptism

It has been said that *"God works in many ways His wonders to perform."* While we can't begin to understand them all, He has revealed many of them.

By His Spirit working through His Word (the Scriptures) and Sacraments, He makes and keeps us His own dear people.

We've read how the Holy Spirit works through the Scriptures, but what are the "Sacraments?"

I. DEFINITION
A Sacrament is a holy rite which has the following Scriptural qualities:
- God Himself commands it.
- Certain Scriptural "means" are connected with God's Word.
- Through a Sacrament, forgiveness of sins is given and sealed.

SO GOD'S WORD TEACHES:
Only Baptism and the Lord's Supper (Holy Communion) have these Scriptural qualities.

II. WHAT IS BAPTISM?
Matthew 28:19 **"Therefore go and make disciples of all nations, baptizing them in the name of the Father and of the Son and of the Holy Spirit"**

Matthew 3:11 (John the Baptist said) "I baptize you with water for repentance. But after me will come one who is more powerful than I, whose sandals I am not fit to carry. He will baptize you with the Holy Spirit and with fire."

SO GOD'S WORD TEACHES:
Baptism is the application of water with the Word of God for personal faith in the Triune God. It is commanded by Christ Himself.

III. THE PURPOSE AND BLESSINGS OF BAPTISM
A. Forgiveness

Acts 2:38 Peter replied, "Repent and be baptized, every one of you, in the name of Jesus Christ for the forgiveness of your sins. And you will receive the gift of the Holy Spirit."

Acts 22:16 "And now what are you waiting for? Get up, be baptized and wash your sins away, calling on his name."

B. Salvation

John 3:5-6 Jesus answered, **"I tell you the truth, no one can enter the kingdom of God unless he is born of water and the Spirit. ⁶Flesh gives birth to flesh, but the Spirit gives birth to spirit."**

Galatians 3:26-27 You are all sons of God through faith in Christ Jesus, ²⁷for all of you who were baptized into Christ have clothed yourselves with Christ.

Mark 16:16 **"Whoever believes and is baptized will be saved, but whoever does not believe will be condemned."**

1 Peter 3:21 (*God's Word Translation*) Baptism doesn't save by removing dirt from the body. Rather, baptism is a request to God for a clear conscience. It saves you through Jesus Christ, who came back from death to life.

Titus 3:5 he saved us, not because of righteous things we had done, but because of his mercy. He saved us through the washing of rebirth and renewal by the Holy Spirit

SO GOD'S WORD TEACHES:

Baptism is God's special way of giving us a new birth, a new identity, a new life! We are freed from sin, guilt, Satan, and death. We are given pardon, life, and salvation. We are adopted into God's family as His children.

IV. SUCH POWERFUL WATER

Eph. 5:25-26 Husbands, love your wives, just as Christ loved the church and gave himself up for her ^{26}to make her holy, cleansing her by the washing with water through the word

SO GOD'S WORD TEACHES:

Baptismal water is plain, ordinary water. It is God's Word that gives the Sacrament of Baptism such great power. The Spirit of God works in this way!

V. A MERE RITUAL?

Mark 16:16 "Whoever believes and is baptized will be saved, but whoever does not believe will be condemned."

Acts 8:35, 36, & 38 Then Philip began with that very passage of Scripture and told him the good news about Jesus. ^{36}As they traveled along the road, they came to some water and the eunuch said, "Look, here is water. Why shouldn't I be baptized?" ^{38}And he gave orders to stop the chariot. Then both Philip and the eunuch went down into the water and Philip baptized him.

Love That Produces a New Birth – Holy Baptism

Acts 2:41 Those who accepted his message were baptized, and about three thousand were added to their number that day.

SO GOD'S WORD TEACHES:
The blessings of Baptism do not come automatically, like the answer from a computer when you have pushed the right keys. They are received only by faith, which is always a gift of the Holy Spirit. Instruction is first given to those who are able to receive it.

VI. IS BAPTISM NECESSARY TO GET TO HEAVEN?
Mark 16:16 "Whoever believes and is baptized will be saved, but whoever does not believe will be condemned."

Luke 23:43 Jesus answered him, "I tell you the truth, today you will be with me in paradise."

Luke 7:30 But the Pharisees and experts in the law rejected God's purpose for themselves, because they had not been baptized by John.

SO GOD'S WORD TEACHES:
Only unbelief damns! Due to various circumstances, some people may die in faith in Christ, but without being baptized. They are in heaven. However, unbelieving rejection of this blessing is fatal rejection of Christ Himself.

VII. BUT AREN'T CHILDREN DIFFERENT?
A. Children's Need
Psalm 51:5 Surely I was sinful at birth, sinful from the time my mother conceived me.

Romans 3:23 for all have sinned and fall short of the glory of God

SO GOD'S WORD TEACHES:
Sinners need forgiveness. All people, including all children, are sinful, naturally separate from God's love. *God's Word* knows nothing of an "age of accountability" or an "age of reason."

B. God's Command

Matthew 28:19 "Therefore go and make disciples of all nations, baptizing them in the name of the Father and of the Son and of the Holy Spirit"

Acts 2:38-39 Peter replied, "Repent and be baptized, every one of you, in the name of Jesus Christ for the forgiveness of your sins. And you will receive the gift of the Holy Spirit. [39]The promise is for you and your children and for all who are far off – for all whom the Lord our God will call."

SO GOD'S WORD TEACHES:
God included children in His plan and command of new birth through Holy Baptism.

C. Can a Child Believe?

Mark 10:13-15 People were bringing little children to Jesus to have him touch them, but the disciples rebuked them. [14]When Jesus saw this, he was indignant. He said to them, **"Let the little children come to me, and do not hinder them, for the kingdom of God belongs to such as these. [15]I tell you the truth, anyone who will not receive the kingdom of God like a little child will never enter it."**

Matthew 18:6 **"But if anyone causes one of these little ones who believe in me to sin, it would be better for him to have a large millstone hung**

around his neck and to be drowned in the depths of the sea."

SO GOD'S WORD TEACHES:
- Children do accept God and trust in Jesus. Their faith is prized by our Lord, and is to be an example for us.
- Every person's faith is a gift of the Holy Spirit (cf. Chapter 4), and we dare not limit Him in giving that gift to only certain people (e.g., adults).
- Baptism is the only means which God has given us to reach infants with His love. Parents should therefore bring their children to Baptism soon after birth (within several weeks).
- *God's Word* says nothing specifically regarding infants who die without Baptism. We are then comforted by knowing that God has bound us – not Himself – to Baptism, and that He wants all to be saved. (cf. Section IX of Chapter 4.)

VIII. SPONSORS OR GOD-PARENTS

Having sponsors is neither commanded in Scripture nor required by the Church. However, it is a good custom of the Church, especially when parents ask sponsors to:
- Witness that the child has been properly baptized.
- Regularly pray for the child.
- Help the child and his/her parents in daily nurturing the new life and faith given in Baptism. To do this, it is obvious that the sponsors must themselves be committed, active Christians. It is preferable that sponsors share the family's own church life.

IX. DAILY VALUE

Galatians 3:27 for all of you who were baptized into Christ have clothed yourselves with Christ.

2 Cor. 5:17 Therefore, if anyone is in Christ, he is a new creation; the old has gone, the new has come!

Eph. 4:24 and to put on the new self, created to be like God in true righteousness and holiness.

SO GOD'S WORD TEACHES:

- Although we are baptized only once, its blessings abide with us throughout life and its meaning should daily deepen.
- Parents should pray with their children and teach them the meaning of their Baptism. They should ask the Church to help via Sunday School and other Christian education agencies.
- Parents should guide and help their children so that their Baptismal blessings are evident to all.

Confirmation in the Lutheran Church is the church-adopted rite in which, after thorough instruction in the basic Christian faith:
- A person publicly professes his/her faith
- Renews his/her Baptismal covenant
- Is admitted to the Lord's Supper

FOOD FOR FURTHER THOUGHT

1. When is your "second birthday?"

2. How could you have a meaningful Baptismal birthday celebration each year?

3. Why aren't Christians re-baptized?

Love That Produces a New Birth – Holy Baptism

4. What is the beauty of Baptism by "immersion?"

5. Explain why Lutheran don't usually "immerse."

6. Mike and Sherry made sure their children, Bob and Kerry, were baptized as infants. Family life was busy, and worship, Sunday School, and other aspects of spiritual life were neglected. – What could you, as a Christian, say and/or do to help them?

7. Your neighbors have children, but refuse to have them baptized or to send them to Sunday School or church. "We had religion shoved down our throats with we were kids, and we're not going to do that to our children," they say. – What is wrong with their thinking?

DAILY GROWTH TROUGH BIBLE READING

1st Day – Luke 8
2nd Day – Luke 9
3rd Day – Luke 10
4th Day – Luke 11
5th Day – Luke 12
6th Day – Luke 13
7th Day – Luke 14

A SCRIPTURAL GEM – For the Memory:

Titus 3:5

He saved us,
    not because of righteous things we had done,
        but because of his mercy.
            He saved us through the washing of rebirth
              and renewal by the Holy Spirit

Chapter 6

Love That Strengthens – the Lord's Supper

It is never enough for a husband and wife to profess their love for each other on their wedding day. It must be repeated and shared regularly for the unity and joy of that marriage. It is not enough for Dad and Mom to become parents – physically. They need to feed, protect, and guide their new infant into maturity.

Our Lord gives and assures us of a new and holy life in Holy Baptism. In the second Sacrament – the Lord's Supper, He nourishes, feeds, and strengthens that new life in Him.

I. **THE SACRAMENT IS GIVEN**

1 Cor. 11:23-25 For I received from the Lord what I also passed on to you: The Lord Jesus, on the night he was betrayed, took bread, [24]and when he had given thanks, he broke it and said, **"This is my body, which is for you; do this in remembrance of me."** [25]In the same way, after supper he took the cup, saying, **"This cup is the new covenant in my blood; do this, whenever you drink it, in remembrance of me."**
cf. Mt. 26:26-28; Mk. 14:22-24; and Lk. 22:19-20

SO GOD'S WORD TEACHES:

On the day before He died for our sins, Jesus ate the Passover meal with His disciples. He then instituted this Sacrament – The Lord's Supper – for the benefit of His Church. Additional names for this Sacrament are: Holy Communion, the Sacrament of the Altar, the Breaking of Bread, and the Eucharist (Thanksgiving).

II. WHAT DOES JESUS GIVE IN THIS SACRAMENT?

Luke 22:19 And he took bread, gave thanks and broke it, and gave it to them, saying, *"This is my body given for you; do this in remembrance of me."*

Matthew 26:27-29 Then he took the cup, gave thanks and offered it to them, saying, *"Drink from it, all of you. 28This is my blood of the covenant, which is poured out for many for the forgiveness of sins. 29I tell you, I will not drink of this fruit of the vine from now on until that day when I drink it anew with you in my Father's kingdom."*

1 Cor. 10:16 Is not the cup of thanksgiving for which we give thanks a participation in the blood of Christ? And is not the bread that we break a participation in the body of Christ?

SO GOD'S WORD TEACHES:

In this Sacrament we receive bread. Jesus used unleavened (without yeast) bread because of the Passover. We also receive wine, the fruit of the vine. With these, Jesus gives us His own body and blood, which was given into death on Calvary. The body and blood of Jesus is really present in, with, and under the bread and wine of Holy Communion.

The following table shows the major different beliefs about the elements of this Sacrament:

	Catholic	Lutheran	Most Protestants
Key Word	changed	is	represents
Present in Sacrament	**only** body and blood	bread & wine **and** body & blood	**only** bread and wine

God's Word does **not** teach that we receive only the bread and wine, which merely serves to remind us of Christ and His sacrifice. This is the teaching of many Protestant churches. Scripture also does **not** teach that the bread and wine are changed into the body and blood of Christ, as the Catholic Church teaches.

III. WHAT ARE WE TO DO WITH THESE ELEMENTS?

1 Cor. 10:16 Is not the cup of thanksgiving for which we give thanks a participation in the blood of Christ? And is not the bread that we break a participation in the body of Christ?

1 Cor. 11:26 For whenever you eat this bread and drink this cup, you proclaim the Lord's death until he comes.

Matthew 26:26-27 "Take and eat; this is my body." ... ²⁷"Drink from it, all of you."

Hebrews 10:14,18 ... by one sacrifice he has made perfect forever those who are being made holy. ... ¹⁸And where these have been forgiven, there is no longer any sacrifice for sin.

SO GOD'S WORD TEACHES:

- We eat and drink the bread and wine naturally, and with them receive Christ's body and blood supernaturally.
- ***All communicants*** are to receive the cup as well as the bread.
- We are not to adore or worship the bread (host), but eat it.
- We are not to re-enact Christ's sacrifice on Calvary in an unbloody manner. Christ's one sacrifice on Calvary is sufficient for all time.

IV. THE BLESSINGS OF THE LORD'S SUPPER

Luke 22:19 And he took bread, gave thanks and broke it, and gave it to them, saying, **"This is my body given for you; do this in remembrance of me."**

2 Cor. 5:15 And he died for all, that those who live should no longer live for themselves but for him who died for them and was raised again.

Matthew 26:28 This is my blood of the covenant, which is poured out for many for the forgiveness of sins.

SO GOD'S WORD TEACHES:
The Lord's Supper is the most personal, intimate, specific way God has of giving us His love to assure us of His continued forgiveness, and of strengthening us in daily Christ-like living.

V. COME OFTEN!

A. God's Command

Luke 22:19 And he took bread, gave thanks and broke it, and gave it to them, saying, **"This is my body given for you; do this in remembrance of me."**

Acts 2:42 They devoted themselves to the apostles' teaching and to the fellowship, to the breaking of bread and to prayer.

SO GOD'S WORD TEACHES:
Our Lord gives us the command, and the early Christian church gives us the example – of frequent attendance at the Lord's Supper.

B. Our Need

Romans 7:19 For what I do is not the good I want to do; no, the evil I do not want to do – this I keep on doing.

SO GOD'S WORD TEACHES:
Even Christians sin daily against God and each other. We need to be reassured of God's continual love.

C. God's Blessing
Luke 22:19 And he took bread, gave thanks and broke it, and gave it to them, saying, **"This is my body given for you; do this in remembrance of me."**
2 Cor. 5:15,17 And he died for all, that those who live should no longer live for themselves but for him who died for them and was raised again. … ¹⁷Therefore, if anyone is in Christ, he is a new creation; the old has gone, the new has come!

SO GOD'S WORD TEACHES:
The Lord's Supper is the most personal way that God uses to continually assure us of His love, pardon, and blessings in our daily life!

D. Our Witness
1 Cor. 11:26 For whenever you eat this bread and drink this cup, you proclaim the Lord's death until he comes.

SO GOD'S WORD TEACHES:
By my presence at the Lord's Supper, I proclaim my faith in Christ with those who have the same faith. It is a witness to His powerful love.

VI. PREPARATION
2 Cor. 13:5 Examine yourselves to see whether you are in the faith; test yourselves. Do you not realize that Christ Jesus is in you – unless, of course, you fail the test?
1 Cor. 11:28-29 A man ought to examine himself before he eats of the bread and drinks of the cup. ²⁹For anyone who eats and drinks without recognizing the body of the Lord eats and drinks judgment on himself.

1 Cor. 10:16 Is not the cup of thanksgiving for which we give thanks a participation in the blood of Christ? And is not the bread that we break a participation in the body of Christ?

Romans 16:17 I urge you, brothers, to watch out for those who cause divisions and put obstacles in your way that are contrary to the teaching you have learned. Keep away from them.

SO GOD'S WORD TEACHES:
- We should regularly evaluate our faith, especially before we partake of this Sacrament, lest we partake of it to our spiritual harm rather than benefit.
- So that none may receive the sacrament to his spiritual harm, it is denied to the impenitent, unforgiving, and uninstructed.

NOTE: Thorough preparation should include answering questions such as:
- Do I believe I have sinned against God and man? How?
- Do I believe Jesus died and rose for me?
- Do I believe He gives me His body and blood for the forgiveness of my sins?
- Do I intend to grow in living more Christ-like each day?

The reading of Scripture – such as Psalm 130, 103, 51, and 32 – is most helpful.

"Registration" for Communion (often done by signing a card in church) is primarily designed to help you prepare yourself to receive the Sacrament in a God-pleasing way.

VII. CELEBRATE!

Luke 22:19 And he took bread, gave thanks and broke it, and gave it to them, saying, **"This is my body given for you; do this in remembrance of me."**

Hebrews 12:2 Let us fix our eyes on Jesus, the author and perfecter of our faith, who for the joy set before him endured the cross, scorning its shame, and sat down at the right hand of the throne of God.

SO GOD'S WORD TEACHES:

Christ's death and our approach to this Sacrament are sorrow-filled because of our sins. I come with a sorrowful, repentant heart. Yet just as Jesus' love in dying for me made that Friday a "Good" Friday, so I rejoice that He still continues to reach out in forgiving, strengthening love to me in this Sacrament. Celebrate! Leave the Lord's Table with genuine joy and thanksgiving for such strengthening love!

FOOD FOR FURTHER THOUGHT

1. Why should *all communicants* receive also the wine in Holy Communion?

2. Why don't Lutherans just use grape juice?

3. When and why should a Christian request "private communion" from his/her pastor?

4. Some people prefer the "common cup" while other prefer the "individual cup." What is the difference?

5. How often should a Christian take Communion?

6. How can an individual Christian show that he/she is actually celebrating the Lord's Supper?

7. Explain why Lutherans do not normally partake of Communion in other churches except in "sister" churches.

8. Christine explained that she didn't go to Communion today because she went to Communion last Sunday. What is wrong with her thinking?

9. Ted is an "inactive alcoholic." Imagine you are Ted's pastor, and Ted tells you he is afraid to drink the wine in Holy Communion. How would you respond to Ted?

DAILY GROWTH THROUGH BIBLE READING

1st Day – Luke 15
2nd Day – Luke 16
3rd Day – Luke 17
4th Day – Luke 18
5th Day – Luke 19
6th Day – Luke 20
7th Day – Luke 21

A SCRIPTURAL GEM – For the Memory:

2 Corinthians 5:15
And he died for all,
   that those who live
      should no longer live for themselves
     but for him
        who died for them and was raised again.

Chapter 7

Love That Gives Us Fellowship – the Church

It is not unusual to feel alone in life, even when there are thousands of other people all around you. God created and redeemed us, however, for fellowship – with Him and with each other. To accomplish this, God has lovingly made us a part of His body, the Church.

I. **THE "INVISIBLE" CHURCH**

Romans 12:5   so in Christ we who are many form one body, and each member belongs to all the others.

Acts 5:14   Nevertheless, more and more men and women believed in the Lord and were added to their number.

Eph. 2:19-22   Consequently, you are no longer foreigners and aliens, but fellow citizens with God's people and members of God's household, [20]built on the foundation of the apostles and prophets, with Christ Jesus himself as the chief cornerstone. [21]In him the whole building is joined together and rises to become a holy temple in the Lord. [22]And in him you too are being built together to become a dwelling in which God lives by his Spirit.

Eph. 4:3-6   Make every effort to keep the unity of the Spirit through the bond of peace. [4]There is one body and one Spirit – just as you were called to one hope when you were called – [5]one Lord, one faith, one baptism; [6]one God and Father of all, who is over all and through all and in all.

Eph. 5:25-27 Husbands, love your wives, just as Christ loved the church and gave himself up for her ^{26}to make her holy, cleansing her by the washing with water through the word, ^{27}and to present her to himself as a radiant church, without stain or wrinkle or any other blemish, but holy and blameless.

1 Cor. 3:11 For no one can lay any foundation other than the one already laid, which is Jesus Christ.

Col. 1:18 And he is the head of the body, the church; he is the beginning and the firstborn from among the dead, so that in everything he might have the supremacy.

SO GOD'S WORD TEACHES:
- Christ is the head of the Church.
- **All** believers and **only** believers in Christ are members of the Church.
- We call the Church "invisible" because only God can look into the heart and know for sure where such faith exists.
- We call the Church the "Communion of Saints," or the "Fellowship of the Forgiven."

NOTE: "The Kingdom of God," "The Bride of Christ," and "The New Jerusalem" are other names given the Church. The term "catholic" (with a small "c") simply means "universal;" the Church is found all over the world – wherever there are believers in Christ.

II. THE VISIBLE CHURCH
A. It's Commission
Matthew 28:19 "Therefore go and make disciples of all nations, baptizing them in the name of the Father and of the Son and of the Holy Spirit."

Matthew 18:18 "I tell you the truth, whatever you bind on earth will be bound in heaven, and

whatever you loose on earth will be loosed in heaven."
Eph. 4:11-12 It was he who gave some to be apostles, some to be prophets, some to be evangelists, and some to be pastors and teachers, ¹²to prepare God's people for works of service, so that the body of Christ may be built up.

SO GOD'S WORD TEACHES:

Those who confess faith in the Triune God are to unite to use the means of grace (Word & Sacraments) for faith-building and evangelism. In His name, they pronounce forgiveness and condemnation.

B. Who Is Responsible?

1 Peter 2:9 But you are a chosen people, a royal priesthood, a holy nation, a people belonging to God, that you may declare the praises of him who called you out of darkness into his wonderful light.

John 20:22-23 And with that he breathed on them and said, **"Receive the Holy Spirit. ²³If you forgive anyone his sins, they are forgiven; if you do not forgive them, they are not forgiven."**

Eph. 4:11-12 It was he who gave some to be apostles, some to be prophets, some to be evangelists, and some to be pastors and teachers, ¹²to prepare God's people for works of service, so that the body of Christ may be built up.

1 Cor. 4:1 So then, men ought to regard us as servants of Christ and as those entrusted with the secret things of God.

2 Cor. 4:5 For we do not preach ourselves, but Jesus Christ as Lord, and ourselves as your servants for Jesus' sake.

Love That Gives Us Fellowship – the Church   63

Col. 4:15 Give my greetings to the brothers at Laodicea, and to Nympha and the church in her house.
Col. 1:28 We proclaim him, admonishing and teaching everyone with all wisdom, so that we may present everyone perfect in Christ.
1 Cor. 14:40 But everything should be done in a fitting and orderly way.

SO GOD'S WORD TEACHES:

- All Christians have the privilege and responsibility for proclaiming the Word and administering the Sacraments. They are to use their various God-given gifts to serve Him and His body.
- Christian congregations, by God's will, call men to be their pastors – spiritual shepherds – who are to train and equip God's people for their service in Christ.

C. Corrective Discipline

Matthew 18:15-18 "If your brother sins against you, go and show him his fault, just between the two of you. If he listens to you, you have won your brother over. [16]But if he will not listen, take one or two others along, so that 'every matter may be established by the testimony of two or three witnesses.' [17]If he refuses to listen to them, tell it to the church; and if he refuses to listen even to the church, treat him as you would a pagan or a tax collector. [18]I tell you the truth, whatever you bind on earth will be bound in heaven, and whatever you loose on earth will be loosed in heaven."

SO GOD'S WORD TEACHES:

When a Christian brother or sister sins openly, we have the responsibility to:
- Use this **progressive procedure:**
  - Talk honestly and personally to him/her.
  - If necessary, take other Christians with you.
  - Tell the local congregation, if necessary, and enlist their help.
  - If the person still refuses to repent, consider that person a "heathen" man or woman. This final act is called *excommunication.*
- Use this **motive** – always genuine, Christian love for the person.
  Hebrews 12:6 (*God's Word Translation*) "The Lord disciplines everyone he loves. He severely disciplines everyone he accepts as his child."
- Have this **goal** – To win him/her back to a living, loving relationship with the Lord. Excommunication is the final Biblical step of love to *shock* the person into the seriousness of his/her sin and seek his/her return to Christ's powerful love.

D. My Relationship With the Visible Church
1. ***It is personal***

   2 Cor. 13:5 Examine yourselves to see whether you are in the faith; test yourselves. Do you not realize that Christ Jesus is in you – unless, of course, you fail the test?

SO GOD'S WORD TEACHES:

Personal faith in Jesus Christ is the basic essential for every church member.

2. The best church for me

1 Peter 4:10-11 Each one should use whatever gift he has received to serve others, faithfully administering God's grace in its various forms. ¹¹If anyone speaks, he should do it as one speaking the very words of God. If anyone serves, he should do it with the strength God provides, so that in all things God may be praised through Jesus Christ. To him be the glory and the power for ever and ever. Amen.

1 Cor. 9:14 In the same way, the Lord has commanded that those who preach the gospel should receive their living from the gospel.

Jeremiah 23:28 "Let the prophet who has a dream tell his dream, but let the one who has my word speak it faithfully. For what has straw to do with grain?" declares the Lord.

Matthew 7:21 "Not everyone who says to me, 'Lord, Lord,' will enter the kingdom of heaven, but only he who does the will of my Father who is in heaven."

Acts 17:11 Now the Bereans were of more noble character than the Thessalonians, for they received the message with great eagerness and examined the Scriptures every day to see if what Paul said was true.

1 Thes. 2:13 And we also thank God continually because, when you received the word of God, which you heard from us, you accepted it not as the word of men, but as it actually is, the word of God, which is at work in you who believe.

Matthew 28:20 "and teaching them to obey everything I have commanded you. And surely I am with you always, to the very end of the age."

SO GOD'S WORD TEACHES:
- The congregation or church which has and faithfully teaches God's Word and administers the Sacraments is the one for me.
- Compare your church's doctrine and pastor's sermons with *God's* Word.
- Don't expect a perfect church. There are hypocrites. Remember that the church is not a gathering of the perfect, but a "hospital for sinners."
- Be a participant, not an observer, in Christian ministry through your church.
- Prayerfully support your pastor, and ask him to equip you for Christian service.

3. *About other church bodies*

1 Cor. 1:10 I appeal to you, brothers, in the name of our Lord Jesus Christ, that all of you agree with one another so that there may be no divisions among you and that you may be perfectly united in mind and thought.

1 John 4:1 Dear friends, do not believe every spirit, but test the spirits to see whether they are from God, because many false prophets have gone out into the world.

Romans 16:17 I urge you, brothers, to watch out for those who cause divisions and put obstacles in your way that are contrary to the teaching you have learned. Keep away from them.

Matthew 7:15 "Watch out for false prophets. They come to you in sheep's clothing, but inwardly they are ferocious wolves."

2 Cor. 6:14-18 Do not be yoked together with unbelievers. For what do righteousness and wickedness have in common? Or what fellowship can light have with darkness? ¹⁵What harmony is there between Christ and Belial? What does a believer have in common with an unbeliever? ¹⁶What agreement is there between the temple of God and idols? For we are the temple of the living God. As God has said: "I will live with them and walk among them, and I will be their God, and they will be my people." ¹⁷"Therefore come out from them and be separate, says the Lord. Touch no unclean thing, and I will receive you." ¹⁸"I will be a Father to you, and you will be my sons and daughters, says the Lord Almighty."

John 5:23 "that all may honor the Son just as they honor the Father. He who does not honor the Son does not honor the Father, who sent him."

Romans 3:28 For we maintain that a man is justified by faith apart from observing the law.

John 16:23 "In that day you will no longer ask me anything. I tell you the truth, my Father will give you whatever you ask in my name."

SO GOD'S WORD TEACHES:

- We rejoice in the common bond of all Christian churches and individuals who are united in faith in the Triune God. We pray and work for greater unity, not mere outward union.
- We are called to be faithful to our Lord and His Word and point out error, and avoid promoting error in any form.
- We especially must be separate from all non-Christian churches, "lodges," or other organizations with religious features which:
  o Deny the Trinity – especially Jesus as God's Son.

- Teach salvation by good works, not by faith in Jesus Christ alone.
- Refrain from praying in Jesus' name in their public prayers.

III. THE STABILITY OF THE CHURCH

Isaiah 55:11 "so is my word that goes out from my mouth: It will not return to me empty, but will accomplish what I desire and achieve the purpose for which I sent it."

Matthew 16:16 Simon Peter answered, "You are the Christ, the Son of the living God."

John 10:27-28 "My sheep listen to my voice; I know them, and they follow me. ^{28}I give them eternal life, and they shall never perish; no one can snatch them out of my hand."

Rev. 11:15 The seventh angel sounded his trumpet, and there were loud voices in heaven, which said: "The kingdom of the world has become the kingdom of our Lord and of his Christ, and he will reign for ever and ever."

SO GOD'S WORD TEACHES:

Until Christ comes the second time, His Word will continue to be proclaimed and His Church will be maintained. No one can change that! Thank God we can be a part of His work on earth.

FOOD FOR FURTHER THOUGHT

1. True or False? – It really doesn't make much difference which church I belong to.

2. True or False? – All believers and only believers belong to "the Church."

3. True or False? – We should expect to have hypocrites in the church.

4. True or False? – There will be people from many church backgrounds in heaven.

5. True or False? – While there are many denominations, there is in reality only one true "Christian" Church.

6. True or False? – Church discipline usually begins on a person-to-person basis.

7. True or False? – The most popular church in town is probably the best church.

8. What are some of the strengths and weaknesses of the "ecumenical" movement?

9. Why do we speak of the "religion of the lodge?"

10. Complete the following:
    o   The most important thing for a church to do is
    _____
    o   God wants me to be active in a church that
    _____

11. According to Scripture, church discipline – including excommunication – can and must be practiced when a person stubbornly persists in sinning. Check all of the following sins for which church discipline may apply:
    _____ Murder   _____ White-collar theft
    _____ Income tax evasion   _____ Gossip
    _____ Hatred/Greed   _____ Adultery
    _____ Un-Biblical divorce   _____ Neglect of public worship
    _____ Cursing

DAILY GROWTH TROUGH BIBLE READING

1st Day – Luke 22
2nd Day – Luke 23
3rd Day – Luke 24
4th Day – Romans 1
5th Day – Romans 2
6th Day – Romans 3
7th Day – Romans 4

A SCRIPTURAL GEM – For the Memory:

Ephesians 4:11-12

It was he who gave
some to be apostles,
some to be prophets,
some to be evangelists,
and some to be pastors and teachers,

[12] to prepare God's people for works of service,
so that the body of Christ may be built up

Chapter 8

Love That Tells It Like It Is – the Bible

God has done and is still doing some fantastic things for us. In addition, He has some exciting plans in store for us. How can we know His love and will? How can we be sure that we are receiving divine guidance and assurance?

I. SOURCE OF OUR KNOWLEDGE
A. Nature

>**Psalm 19:1** The heavens declare the glory of God; the skies proclaim the work of his hands.
>
>**Romans 1:19-20** … since what may be known about God is plain to them, because God has made it plain to them. [20]For since the creation of the world God's invisible qualities – his eternal power and divine nature – have been clearly seen, being understood from what has been made, so that men are without excuse.

SO GOD'S WORD TEACHES:

We can learn from nature and from our conscience that there is a God who is wise and powerful and to whom we are accountable. The natural knowledge of God does not, however, tell us specifically who this powerful and wise God is.

B. Revelation

>**Isaiah 42:8** "I am the Lord; that is my name! I will not give my glory to another or my praise to idols."

John 17:3 "This is eternal life: that they may know you, the only true God, and Jesus Christ, whom you have sent."

John 17:17 "your word is truth." (Jesus said to the Father)

Acts 17:23-24 As I walk around and observe your objects of worship, I even found an altar with this inscription: TO AN UNKNOWN GOD. Now what you worship as something unknown I am going to proclaim to you. [24]The God who made the world and everything in it is the Lord of heaven and earth and does not live in temples built by hands.

SO GOD'S WORD TEACHES:

God Himself tells (reveals) His love and will to us in His Word, the Bible.

II. GOD'S WORD

A. How We Got God's Word – the Bible

2 Tim. 3:16 All Scripture is God-breathed.

2 Peter 1:21 For prophecy never had its origin in the will of man, but men spoke from God as they were carried along by the Holy Spirit.

1 Cor. 2:13 This is what we speak, not in words taught us by human wisdom but in words taught by the Spirit, expressing spiritual truths in spiritual words.

SO GOD'S WORD TEACHES:

God gave us His Word by inspiration. *"Inspiration"* is the process by which God so directed the sacred writers that what they wrote was fully His Word. This includes each word and every book of the Bible as originally written.

B. The Format of God's Word – the Bible

	Old Testament	New Testament	Entire Bible
Books	39	3×9 = 27	66
Language	Hebrew	Greek	
Time	1500 BC -- *about 1600 years* -- AD 100		
Authors	About 40		

C. The Center of God's Word – the Bible

John 5:39 "You diligently study the Scriptures because you think that by them you possess eternal life. These are the Scriptures that testify about me." (Jesus is speaking.)

Acts 10:43 All the prophets testify about him that everyone who believes in him receives
forgiveness of sins through his name.

John 20:31 But these are written that you may believe that Jesus is the Christ, the Son of God, and that by believing you may have life in his name.

SO GOD'S WORD TEACHES:
Jesus Christ is the center and focal point of all Scripture. The Old Testament points ahead to Jesus as the coming Messiah. The New Testament reveals His coming, living, dying, rising – to be our Savior.

D. The Reliability and Authority of Scripture

John 17:17 "Your word is truth." (Jesus said to the Father.)

John 10:35 "… and the Scripture cannot be broken …"

Rev. 22:18-19 I warn everyone who hears the words of the prophecy of this book: If anyone adds anything to them, God will add to him the plagues described in this book. [19]And if anyone takes words away from this book of prophecy, God will take away from him his share in the tree of life and in the holy city, which are described in this book.

Mt. 5:18 "I tell you the truth, until heaven and earth disappear, not the smallest letter, not the least stroke of a pen, will by any means disappear from the Law until everything is accomplished."

Titus 1:2-3 … a faith and knowledge resting on the hope of eternal life, which God, who does not lie, promised before the beginning of time, [3]and at his appointed season he brought his word to light through the preaching entrusted to me by the command of God our Savior.

SO GOD'S WORD TEACHES:

Since the Bible is God's inspired Word, it is without error and is absolutely reliable in all it says – from "spiritual" matters to geographical, historical, and scientific matters. We are not to add or subtract anything regarding the Scriptures.

E. Scripture's Main Teachings

Leviticus 19:2 Speak to the entire assembly of Israel and say to them: "Be holy because I, the Lord your God am holy."

Romans 1:16 I am not ashamed of the gospel, because it is the power of God for the salvation of everyone who believes.

Romans 3:20 Therefore no one will be declared righteous in his sight by observing the law; rather, through the law we become conscious of sin.

Romans 6:23 For the wages of sin is death.

1 John 4:9 This is how God showed his love among us: He sent his one and only Son into the world that we might live through him.

John 3:16 "For God so loved the world that he gave his one and only son that whoever believes in him should not perish but have eternal life."

Psalm 119:105 Your word is a lamp to my feet and a light for my path.

2 Cor. 5:14-15 For Christ's love compels us ... ¹⁵And he died for all, that those who live should no longer live for themselves but for him who died for them and was raised again.

Phil. 4:13 I can do everything through him who gives me strength.

	LAW	GOSPEL
Content	Tells what *we* are to do and to avoid – Lev. 19:2	Tells what *God* does for us, for our salvation – Rom. 1:16
Effects	*Shows us*: 1. Our *sin* – Rom. 3:20 2. God's *anger* and *punishment* – Rom. 6:23	*Shows us*: 1. Our *Savior* – 1 John 4:9 2. God's amazing *grace* – John 3:16
Application	To *everyone*, especially to *those not sorry* for their sins	To troubled and *repentant sinners*
For Christians	*Directs* Christian living – Psalm 119:105	*Motivates* Christian living – 2 Cor. 5:14-15 *Empowers* Christian living – Phil. 4:13

F. The Purposes of Scripture

2 Tim. 3:15-17 and how from infancy you have known the holy Scriptures, which are able to make you wise for salvation through faith in Christ Jesus. ¹⁶All Scripture is God-breathed and is useful for teaching, rebuking, correcting and training in righteousness, ¹⁷so that the servant of God may be thoroughly equipped for every good work.

Psalm 119:105 Your word is a lamp to my feet and a light for my path.

SO GOD'S WORD TEACHES:

The purposes of God's Word, the Scriptures, may be summarized in this way:
- To give us salvation through faith in Christ as our Savior
- To train and equip us for Christ-like living

G. Use Your Bible!

John 5:39 "You diligently study the Scriptures because you think that by them you possess eternal life. These are the Scriptures that testify about me"

Luke 11:28 He replied, "Blessed rather are those who hear the word of God and obey it."

Luke 2:19 But Mary treasured up all these things and pondered them in her heart.

John 14:23 Jesus replied, "If anyone loves me, he will obey my teaching. My Father will love him, and we will come to him and make our home with him."

Acts 4:20 "For we cannot help speaking about what we have seen and heard."

SO GOD'S WORD TEACHES:

We are to study, believe, live and share God's precious Word each day. What blessings God has in store for us through His Word! As you read the Bible daily, ask yourself:
- What is it saying?
- What does it mean?
- How should it help me in my life in the Lord?

FOOD FOR FURTHER THOUGHT

1. True or False? – It is un-natural to be an atheist.

2. True or False? – The Bible tells us all we'll ever need to know for our salvation.

3. True or False? – The Law is only in the Old Testament, and the Gospel is only in the New Testament.

4. True or False? – The Law never saves; only the Gospel can save, motivate, and give power.

5. True or False? – The main theme of the Old Testament is Jesus Christ.

6. True or False? – We may properly say: "God is THE author of the Bible."

7. True or False? – The Bible is a reliable guide for twentieth century Christian living – including marriage, money, family, etc.

8. True or False? – Since the Bible's main purpose is to tell us God's love, it may include mistakes when it deals with geographical locations or scientific notations.

9. True or False? – The Bible may contain minor mistakes since its words were written by men.

10. True or False? – The King James version is the official version of the Bible.

11. What is the difference between a "translation" and a "paraphrase?"

DAILY GROWTH TROUGH BIBLE READING

1st Day – Romans 5
2nd Day – Romans 6
3rd Day – Romans 7
4th Day – Romans 8
5th Day – Romans 9
6th Day – Romans 10
7th Day – Romans 11

A SCRIPTURAL GEM – For the Memory:

2 Timothy 3:16-17
All Scripture is God-breathed
and is useful for
teaching,
 rebuking,
  correcting,
   and training in righteousness,

[17] so that the servant of God
may be thoroughly equipped
for every good work.

Chapter 9

Love That Directs Life – Toward God
† 1ˢᵗ Commandment †

You bought a new car. You admire its beauty. You're sure it will provide reliable transportation. It is absolutely essential that you actually get into your car and drive it if you are to realize the value of your investment.

Christianity is not only something you believe or possess, but something you live. Christianity is not only who you are in Christ, but how you live in Christ. In Chapter 4 we studied how the Holy Spirit gives us new life through faith in Jesus Christ. We now examine more closely how that new life is lived.

I. RESULTS EXPECTED

Eph. 2:10 For we are God's workmanship, created in Christ Jesus to do good works, which God prepared in advance for us to do.

James 2:26 … so faith without deeds is dead.

1 Cor. 10:13 So whether you eat or drink or whatever you do, do it all for the glory of God.

SO GOD'S WORD TEACHES:

Our Lord expects our lives to be fruitful and useful as they are lived according to His will for us. The Ten Commandments is God's moral code of conduct for us to follow in our daily living so that He might be glorified and that our lives might be joyful and useful. In the Commandments, our Lord tells us what we ***should do*** and what we ***should avoid doing***. While not every possible question regarding Christian conduct is specifically answered in God's Word, these Commandments and related Scriptures are given to direct our lives in loving service to God and other people.

II. WHY LIVE THE CHRISTIAN LIFE?

2 Cor. 5:14-15 For Christ's love compels us, because we are convinced that one died for all, and therefore all died. ¹⁵And he died for all, that those who live should no longer live for themselves but for him who died for them and was raised again.

John 14:15 "If you love me, you will obey what I command."

Galatians 5:13 You, my brothers, were called to be free. But do not use your freedom to indulge in the sinful nature; rather serve one another in love.

Romans 13:10 Love does no harm to its neighbor. Therefore love is the fulfillment of the Law.

Galatians 5:6 For in Christ Jesus neither circumcision nor uncircumcision has any value. The only thing that counts is faith expressing itself through love.

Hebrews 11:6 without faith it is impossible to please God

John 15:5 "I am the vine; you are the branches. If a man remains in me and I in him, he will bear much fruit; apart from me you can do nothing."

SO GOD'S WORD TEACHES:

God's love in Christ is the Christian's motive and power to obey God's will. Christians do not do good or live right in order to earn either God's favor or man's praise. As Christians, our lives are a "thanks-living," a grateful response to our God of love.

III. THE OUTLINE
Matthew 22:37 "Love the Lord your God with all your heart and with all your soul and with all your mind."
Matthew 22:39 "Love your neighbor as yourself."

SO GOD'S WORD TEACHES:
- The first 3 Commandments (1-3) tell what God expects of us in our relationship *to Him*.
- The last 7 Commandments (4-10) tell what God expects of us in our relationship *to others*.

NOTE: Some denominations number the Commandments differently, but this does not change the Word of God or its meaning.

IV. THE FIRST COMMANDMENT: Exodus 20:3 "You shall have no other gods before me."
A. We Should Honor
Matthew 4:10 "Worship the Lord your God and serve him only."
Matthew 22:37 "Love the Lord your God with all your heart and with all your soul and with all your mind."
Matthew 6:10 "Your will be done on earth as it is in heaven."
Proverbs 3:5 Trust in the Lord with all your heart and lean not on your own understanding.
Psalm 73:25-26 Whom have I in heaven but you? And earth has nothing I desire besides you. [26]My flesh and my heart may fail, but God is the strength of my heart and my portion forever.
1 Cor. 10:31 So whether you eat or drink or whatever you do, do it all for the glory of God.
Matthew 16:24 "If anyone would come after me, he must deny himself and take up his cross and follow me."

SO GOD'S WORD TEACHES:
The Triune God is to be "Number 1" in every aspect of our lives – in value, importance, thinking, planning, doing, and even suffering. Our goal is to honor Him in our work, marriage, home-life, business, leisure activities, and financial affairs.

B. We Should Witness

Matthew 28:19-20 "Therefore go and make disciples of all nations, baptizing them in the name of the Father and of the Son and of the Holy Spirit, [20] and teaching them to obey everything I have commanded you."

Acts 1:8 "you will receive power when the Holy Spirit comes on you; and you will be my witnesses in Jerusalem, and in all Judea and Samaria, and to the ends of the earth."

Matthew 6:10 "your kingdom come"

1 Peter 3:15 Always be prepared to give an answer to everyone who asks you to give the reason for the hope that you have.

1 Peter 2:9 You are a chosen people, a royal priesthood, a holy nation, a people belonging to God, that you may declare the praises of him who called you out of darkness into his wonderful light.

Matthew 5:16 "In the same way, let your light shine before men, that they may see your good deeds and praise your Father in heaven."

SO GOD'S WORD TEACHES:
It is the highest privilege and greatest responsibility of every Christian to share his Christian faith with unbelievers. We call this sharing "witnessing," "evangelism," or "mission work." We are to begin this witnessing with our own family and friends, continually

Love That Directs Life – Toward God
† *1ˢᵗ Commandment* †

reaching out in love to tell others about our God who loves them and has redeemed them.

C. We Should Avoid

Isaiah 42:8 "I am the Lord; that is my name! I will not give my glory to another or my praise to idols."

John 5:23 "That all may honor the Son just as they honor the Father. He who does not honor the Son does not honor the Father who sent him."

Matthew 10:37 "Anyone who loves his father more than me is not worthy of me; anyone who loves his son or daughter more than me is not worthy of me."

Proverbs 3:5 Trust in the Lord with all your heart and lean not on your own understanding.

Mark 10:24-25 The disciples were amazed at his words. But Jesus said again, "Children, how hard it is to enter the kingdom of God. ²⁵It is easier for a camel to go through the eye of a needle than for a rich man to enter the kingdom of God."

Phil. 3:19 Their destiny is destruction, their god is their stomach, and their glory is their shame. Their mind is on earthly things.

Ephesians 5:5 For of this you can be sure: No immoral, impure or greedy person – such a man is an idolater – has any inheritance in the kingdom of Christ and of God.

SO GOD'S WORD TEACHES:

We are *not* to have any god besides the Triune God. If anyone denies Jesus as God's Son and his/her Savior, neither will God the Father accept his/her worship. The worship of a false god is idolatry. Everyone has a god, for whoever or whatever is *most important* to you is your god.

FOOD FOR FURTHER THOUGHT

1. Why is love, rather than fear, the Christian motivation for life?
2. List some of the popular false gods of our world today.
3. What connection does getting married or choosing a job have with the First Commandment?
4. Discuss: *"If we keep the First Commandment perfectly, we wouldn't need the other nine."*
5. When we witness for our Lord, what is the most important thing to share?
6. Name one person to whom you will – with God's help – witness, beginning this week.
7. Can an unbeliever do good works, acceptable to God?
8. True or False? – As long as a Christian does not sin "terribly" – like sins of theft, lying, adultery, or murder – his life can be considered rather successful.
9. Explain why money, family, or job can so easily become a false god to us.

DAILY GROWTH TROUGH BIBLE READING

1st Day – Romans 12
2nd Day – Romans 13
3rd Day – Romans 14
4th Day – Romans 15
5th Day – Romans 16
6th Day – 1 Corinthians 1
7th Day – 1 Corinthians 2

A SCRIPTURAL GEM – For the Memory:

John 14:15
"If you love me, you will obey what I command."

Chapter 10

Love That Directs Life – Toward God
† 2nd & 3rd Commandments †

The First Commandment sets the pace for all the others. Because God's person and position are so important, so also are His name and worship.

What wonderful opportunities to show how we love Him are given to us in the 2nd and 3rd Commandments!

I. **THE SECOND COMMANDMENT: Exodus 20:7** "You shall not misuse the name of the LORD your God"
   A. **Definition**
      Isaiah 42:8 "I am the Lord; that is my name! I will not give my glory to another or my praise to idols."
      Matthew 1:21 "She will give birth to a son, and you are to give him the name Jesus, because he will save his people from their sins."
      Exodus 20:24 "Make an altar of earth for me and sacrifice on it your burnt offerings and fellowship offerings, your sheep and goats and your cattle. Wherever I cause my name to be honored, I will come to you and bless you."

SO GOD'S WORD TEACHES:
- God's name consists not only of the "proper nouns" (for example, "Lord, Father, Jesus, Spirit"), but includes everything through which He tells us of Himself.
    - Compare the Baptismal "formula."

B. We Should Praise and Thank

Psalm 103:1   Praise the LORD, O my soul; all my inmost being, praise his holy name.

Ephesians 5:20   … always giving thanks to God the Father for everything, in the name of our Lord Jesus Christ.

Luke 17:15-16   One of them, when he saw he was healed, came back, praising God in a loud voice. ¹⁶He threw himself at Jesus' feet and thanked him – and he was a Samaritan.

SO GOD'S WORD TEACHES:

All Christians should regularly, joyfully, and thankfully speak of the goodness of the Lord – to Him and to other people. If others hear the name of Jesus from our lips, it should be a "compliment" to our God.

B. We Should Ask In Prayer
1. Why Pray?

Psalm 50:15   "call upon me in the day of trouble; I will deliver you, and you will honor me."

Matthew 7:7   **"Ask and it will be given to you; seek and you will find; knock and the door will be opened to you."**

Phil. 4:6   Do not be anxious about anything, but in everything, by prayer and petition, with thanksgiving, present your requests to God.

1 Thes. 5:17   pray continually

SO GOD'S WORD TEACHES:

God wants us to talk with Him in prayer regularly and frequently, including when we have a need of any kind.

2. How Should I Pray?

Matthew 6:7 "And when you pray, do not keep on babbling like pagans, for they think they will be heard because of their many words."

Matthew 6:6 "But when you pray, go into your room, close the door and pray to your Father, who is unseen. Then your Father, who sees what is done in secret, will reward you."

John 16:23 "I tell you the truth, my Father will give you whatever you ask in my name."

1 Tim. 2:1-2 I urge, then, first of all, that requests, prayers, intercession and thanksgiving be made for everyone – ²for kings and all those in authority, that we may live peaceful and quiet lives in all godliness and holiness.

Hebrews 9:27 Just as man is destined to die once, and after that to face judgment,

James 1:6-7 But when he asks, he must believe and not doubt, because he who doubts is like a wave of the sea, blown and tossed by the wind. ⁷That man should not think he will receive anything from the Lord.

Luke 11:13 "If you then, though you are evil, know how to give good gifts to your children, how much more will your Father in heaven give the Holy Spirit to those who ask him!"

Matthew 8:2 A man with leprosy came and knelt before him and said, "Lord, if you are willing, you can make me clean."

SO GOD'S WORD TEACHES:

God's children delight in coming to their dear Heavenly Father in prayer:
- Not merely repeating or reciting words
- Humbly and sincerely

- For all people
- In Jesus' name, who opened the door to our Father's heart
- In faith and confidence
- Asking for spiritual blessings without reservation
- Asking for temporal blessings (those of value for this life only) according to His divine wisdom and powerful love.
- Not praying for "the dead," whose souls are either already with Christ or already forever separated from His love

   3. ***Expect God to Hear and Answer Your Prayers***
   Isaiah 65:24 "Before they call I will answer; while they are still speaking I will hear."
   Matthew 7:8 **"For everyone who asks receives; he who seeks finds; and to him who knocks, the door will be opened."**
   Matthew 11:28 **"Come to me, all you who are weary and burdened, and I will give you rest."**
   2 Cor. 12:8-9 Three times I pleaded with the Lord to take it away from me. ⁹But he said to me, "My grace is sufficient for you, for my power is made perfect in weakness." Therefore I will boast all the more gladly about my weaknesses, so that Christ's power may rest on me.
   John 2:4 **"Dear woman, why do you involve me?"** Jesus replied. **"My time has not yet come."**

SO GOD'S WORD TEACHES:

God answers every time His children call on His name. His answer is always one of love for us. Sometimes He says "Yes," other times "No," and still other times "Wait" or "I'll substitute."

Love That Directs Life – Toward God
† 2nd & 3rd Commandments †

C. **We Should Avoid:**

   1. *Degrading God's Name*

      Exodus 20:7 "You shall not misuse the name of the LORD your God, for the LORD will not hold anyone guiltless who misuses his name."

   2. *Cursing*

      James 3:9-10 With the tongue we praise our Lord and Father, and with it we curse men, who have been made in God's likeness. ¹⁰Out of the same mouth come praise and cursing. My brothers, this should not be.

   3. *Sinful Swearing*

      Matthew 5:34-37 "But I tell you, Do not swear at all: either by heaven, for it is God's throne; ³⁵or by the earth, for it is his footstool; or by Jerusalem, for it is the city of the Great King. ³⁶And do not swear by your head, for you cannot make even one hair white or black. ³⁷Simply let your 'Yes' be 'Yes,' and your 'No,' 'No;' anything beyond this comes from the evil one.

   4. *Witchcraft, Astrology, etc.*

      Leviticus 19:31 "Do not turn to mediums or seek out spiritists, for you will be defiled by them. I am the LORD your God."

   5. *False Prophets*

      Jeremiah 23:31 "Yes," declares the LORD, "I am against the prophets who wag their own tongues and yet declare, 'The LORD declares.'"

6. *Hypocrisy*
Matthew 7:21 "Not everyone who says to me, 'Lord, Lord,' will enter the kingdom of heaven, but only he who does the will of my Father who is in heaven."

II. THE THIRD COMMANDMENT: Exodus 20:8
"Remember the Sabbath day by keeping it holy."

A. The Subject

Col. 2:16-17 Therefore do not let anyone judge you by what you eat or drink, or with regard to a religious festival, a New Moon celebration or a Sabbath day. ^{17}These are a shadow of the things that were to come; the reality, however, is found in Christ.

Romans 14:6 He who regards one day as special, does so to the Lord. He who eats meat, eats to the Lord, for he gives thanks to God; and he who abstains, does so to the Lord and gives thanks to God.

Galatians 4:10-11 You are observing special days and months and seasons and years! ^{11}I fear for you, that somehow I have wasted my efforts on you.

SO GOD'S WORD TEACHES:

The Old Testament "Ceremonial Law" required God's people to worship *on the seventh day of the week (Saturday)* in very specific ways. This pointed to the coming Messiah. For New Testament Christians, the 3rd Commandment speaks of worship without those detailed ceremonial specifications since the Messiah – Jesus – had already come to earth!

B. We Should Worship the Lord

Psalm 26:8 I love the house where you live, O Lord, the place where your glory dwells.

Love That Directs Life – Toward God
† 2nd & 3rd Commandments †

Col. 3:16 Let the word of Christ dwell in you richly as you teach and admonish one another with all wisdom, and as you sing psalms, hymns and spiritual songs with gratitude in your hearts to God.

John 8:47 **"He who belongs to God hears what God says. The reason you do not hear is that you do not belong to God."**

1 Thes. 2:13 And we also thank God continually because, when you received the word of God, which you heard from us, you accepted it not as the word of men, but as it actually is, the word of God, which is at work in you who believe.

Luke 11:28 He replied, **"Blessed rather are those who hear the word of God and obey it."**

Acts 2:42 They devoted themselves to the apostles' teaching and to the fellowship, to the breaking of bread and to prayer.

SO GOD'S WORD TEACHES:

Worship is neither optional nor a burdensome task for the Christian. Rather it is his regular opportunity to confess his sin, sing God's praise, hear the Word of the Lord, and be strengthened for daily service. Worship is welcomed by sincere Christians!

WORSHIP NOTE:
- Worship is *two-way* communication:
  - *God speaks to us* through the Word – Scripture lessons, the Absolution, parts of the liturgy, and the Sacraments.
  - *We speak to God* in our songs, prayers, and parts of the liturgy.
- Corporate worship is not a gathering of the perfect, but a gathering of sinners seeking pardon, guidance, and strength from their Lord.

- **Our worship generally follows a yearly pattern**:
  - *Festival Half*
    - Advent – 4 weeks, beginning about December 1st, when we recall the Old Testament promises of the coming Messiah and prepare to celebrate their fulfillment in Jesus' birth.
    - Christmas – We celebrate God our Father, who in love gave the world His Son. That Son is Jesus, conceived by the Holy Spirit and born of the Virgin Mary.
    - Epiphany – January 6th – We celebrate the Gospel as God's powerful gift of love for everyone, everywhere.
    - Lent – 40 days before Easter – focuses on our repentance and Christ's atonement. It culminates in *Holy Week*, especially *Maundy Thursday*, when Jesus instituted the Lord's Supper, and *Good Friday*, when He was crucified.
    - Easter – We celebrate the Resurrection of Jesus Christ from the dead, assuring us of eternal life with Him.
    - Ascension – 40 days after Easter – when Jesus ascended to the Father
    - Pentecost – 50 days after Easter – celebrating the out-pouring of the Holy Spirit on the early Church
    - Trinity Sunday – emphasizes the Biblical teaching of One God in three persons

  - *Non-Festival Half*
    During the last six months of the church year, there are no major festivals. The Scripture lessons focus on our living and sharing our faith on a daily basis – individually and as His body, the Church.

C. We Should Support the Proclaiming of the Word

Hebrews 13:17 Obey your leaders and submit to their authority. They keep watch over you as men who must give an account. Obey them so that their work will be a joy, not a burden, for that would be of no advantage to you.

Galatians 6:6 Anyone who receives instruction in the word must share all good things with his instructor.

1 Tim. 5:17 The elders who direct the affairs of the church well are worthy of double honor, especially those whose work is preaching and teaching.

SO GOD'S WORD TEACHES:

Christians support and honor their pastors and others who proclaim the Gospel as God's servants. We should give prayer, verbal, and financial support to their labors in the Lord.

D. We Should Avoid *"Worship Abuse"*

John 8:47 "He who belongs to God hears what God says. The reason you do not hear is that you do not belong to God."

Luke 10:16 "He who listens to you listens to me; he who rejects you rejects me; but he who rejects me rejects him who sent me."

Hebrews 10:25 Let us not give up meeting together, as some are in the habit of doing, but let us encourage one another – and all the more as you see the Day approaching.

Eccles. 5:1 Guard your steps when you go to the house of God. Go near to listen rather than to offer the sacrifice of fools, who do not know that they do wrong.

SO GOD'S WORD TEACHES:
We should *not neglect* regular worship, nor should we come with a *careless attitude.* Neglect of Word and Sacrament dishonors God and robs us of spiritual nourishment.

FOOD FOR FURTHER THOUGHT

1. Is it really wrong to pray for earthy things like sunshine for a picnic, a raise in pay, or a good grade in school?

2. Why should we not pray to "saints" – or for people who have already died?

3. "Faith healing" often implies God will physically heal all who "really believe." What is wrong with this thinking?

4. Make a "prayer list" for this week, praying by name for a different person each day.

5. Can you explain why so many people have a hard time "getting to church."

6. What are "family devotions" and why are they so important?

7. Do you have or will you begin a habit of reading the Word of God daily – at least 10 minutes per day?

8. Why do most Christians prefer Sunday as their favorite day to worship?

9. What difference does it make what "order of worship" or "liturgy" we use?

Love That Directs Life – Toward God
✝ *2ⁿᵈ & 3ʳᵈ Commandments* ✝

DAILY GROWTH TROUGH BIBLE READING

1st Day – 1 Corinthians 3
2nd Day – 1 Corinthians 4
3rd Day – 1 Corinthians 5
4th Day – 1 Corinthians 6
5th Day – 1 Corinthians 7
6th Day – 1 Corinthians 8
7th Day – 1 Corinthians 9

A SCRIPTURAL GEM – For the Memory:

Philippians 4:6
Do not be anxious about anything,
  but in everything,
    by prayer and petition,
      with thanksgiving,
        present your requests to God.

Chapter 11

Love That Directs Life – Toward Others
† 4th – 6th Commandments †

God loves us very much. He wants His love for us to motivate us to love and serve not only Him, but also our neighbor. Our neighbors are, very simply, people – people all around us – all in need of our love.

I. THE GENERAL PRINCIPLE

Galatians 6:10 Therefore, as we have opportunity, let us do good to all people, especially to those who belong to the family of believers.

1 John 4:20 If anyone says, "I love God," yet hates his brother, he is a liar. For anyone who does not love his brother, whom he has seen, cannot love God, whom he has not seen.

SO GOD'S WORD TEACHES:

We show, and others see, God's love in and through our actions and lives.

II. THE FOURTH COMMANDMENT: Exodus 20:12 "Honor your father and your mother, so that you may live long in the land the LORD your God is giving you."

A. We Should Honor Authorities

Ephesians 6:2 "Honor your father and mother" – which is the first commandment with a promise

Leviticus 19:32 "Rise in the presence of the aged, show respect for the elderly and revere your God. I am the LORD."

Love That Directs Life – Toward Others
† 4th – 6th Commandments †

1 Tim. 5:4 But if a widow has children or grandchildren, these should learn first of all to put their religion into practice by caring for their own family and so repaying their parents and grandparents, for this is pleasing to God.

Romans 13:6 This is also why you pay taxes, for the authorities are God's servants, who give their full time to governing.

1 Peter 2:13-14 Submit yourselves for the Lord's sake to every authority instituted among men: whether to the king, as the supreme authority, [14]or to governors, who are sent by him to punish those who do wrong and to commend those who do right.

1 Peter 2:18 Slaves, submit yourselves to your masters with all respect, not only to those who are good and considerate, but also to those who are harsh.

Ephesians 6:5-7 Slaves, obey your earthly masters with respect and fear, and with sincerity of heart, just as you would obey Christ. [6]Obey them not only to win their favor when their eye is on you, but like slaves of Christ, doing the will of God from your heart. [7]Serve wholeheartedly, as if you were serving the Lord, not men.

SO GOD'S WORD TEACHES:

God has placed different people in authority over us in various areas of life, beginning with our parents in the home. We are to honor them as God's servants through whom He guides and blesses us in various areas and times of our earthly life. We should work with them and obey them in the areas over which God has placed them in our lives.

B. We Should Honor God First

Acts 5:29 Peter and the other apostles replied: "We must obey God rather than men!"

SO GOD'S WORD TEACHES:
God's will must always take priority over the will of any and every person or organization.

C. We Should Avoid

Proverbs 30:17 "The eye that mocks a father, that scorns obedience to a mother, will be pecked out by the ravens of the valley, will be eaten by the vultures."

Romans 13:2 Consequently, he who rebels against the authority is rebelling against what God has instituted, and those who do so will bring judgment on themselves.

SO GOD'S WORD TEACHES:
God will punish those who disregard His plan for order and security in society, as well as those who dishonor His representatives in the home and other levels of society.

III. THE FIFTH COMMANDMENT: Exodus 20:13 "You shall not murder."

A. We Should Promote Life

Matthew 5:5,7,9 "Blessed are the meek, for they will inherit the earth. ... ⁷Blessed are the merciful, for they will be shown mercy. ... ⁹Blessed are the peacemakers, for they will be called sons of God."

Ephesians 4:32 Be kind and compassionate to one another, forgiving each other, just as in Christ God forgave you.

Matthew 25:35-36,40 "For I was hungry and you gave me something to eat, I was thirsty and you gave me something to drink, I was a stranger and

Love That Directs Life – Toward Others
† *4th – 6th Commandments* †

you invited me in, 36I needed clothes and you clothed me, I was sick and you looked after me, I was in prison and you came to visit me." ... 40 ... 'I tell you the truth, whatever you did for one of the least of these brothers of mine, you did for me.'"
Matthew 6:15 "**But if you do not forgive men their sins, your Father will not forgive your sins.**"
Romans 12:20 On the contrary: "If your enemy is hungry, feed him; if he is thirsty, give him something to drink. In doing this, you will heap burning coals on his head."

SO GOD'S WORD TEACHES:

In genuine Christian love, we are to reach out to our neighbor in his physical and personal needs. This includes forgiveness. It even reaches out to our enemies.

B. We Should Avoid

Genesis 9:6 "Whoever sheds the blood of man, by man shall his blood be shed; for in the image of God has God made man."
Job 1:21 (Job said) "Naked I came from my mother's womb, and naked I will depart. The LORD gave and the LORD has taken away; may the name of the LORD be praised."
1 John 3:15 Anyone who hates his brother is a murderer, and you know that no murderer has eternal life in him.
Matthew 15:19 "**For out of the heart come evil thoughts, murder, adultery, sexual immorality, theft, false testimony, slander.**"

SO GOD'S WORD TEACHES:

Murder, suicide, nearly all abortions, genocide, "mercy killing" (euthanasia), physical harm, hatred, bitterness, or any other method of destroying or hurting God-given life is wrong. Christians are to obey God's will rather than do whatever society allows.

C. The Scriptural Exception

Matthew 26:52 "Put your sword back in its place," Jesus said to him, "for all who draw the sword will die by the sword."

Romans 13:4 For he is God's servant to do you good. But if you do wrong, be afraid, for he does not bear the sword for nothing. He is God's servant, an agent of wrath to bring punishment on the wrongdoer.

SO GOD'S WORD TEACHES:

God has delegated to the government the responsibility to govern, including the punishing of evil-doers. This includes capital punishment and "just" wars. Christians may indeed serve their country and God in these ways.

IV. THE SIXTH COMMANDMENT: Exodus 20:14 "You shall not commit adultery."

A. God's View of Sexuality

Genesis 1:27,31 So God created man in his own image, in the image of God he created him; male and female he created them. ... ³¹God saw all that he had made, and it was very good. And there was evening, and there was morning – the sixth day.

Matthew 19:6 "So they are no longer two, but one. Therefore what God has joined together, let man not separate."

SO GOD'S WORD TEACHES:

Both human sexuality and marriage are God-given gifts, and therefore very good gifts.

Love That Directs Life – Toward Others
† *4th – 6th Commandments* †

B. We Should Use Sexuality and Marriage Positively

Genesis 2:18 The LORD God said, "It is not good for the man to be alone. I will make a helper suitable for him."

Genesis 1:28 God blessed them and said to them, "Be fruitful and increase in number; fill the earth and subdue it. Rule over the fish of the sea and the birds of the air and over every living creature that moves on the ground."

1 Cor. 7:2 But since there is so much immorality, each man should have his own wife, and each woman her own husband.

1 Cor. 6:19 Do you not know that your body is a temple of the Holy Spirit, who is in you, whom you have received from God? You are not your own.

Phil. 4:8 Finally, brothers, whatever is true, whatever is noble, whatever is right, whatever is pure, whatever is lovely, whatever is admirable – if anything is excellent or praiseworthy – think about such things.

Ephesians 5:24-25 Now as the church submits to Christ, so also wives should submit to their husbands in everything. ²⁵Husbands, love your wives, just as Christ loved the church and gave himself up for her

SO GOD'S WORD TEACHES:
- We should recognize and use marriage and sexual intercourse within marriage for the blessings God intended: companionship, sharing, procreation, and avoiding immorality.
- We should recognize our bodies as God's temple and use our thoughts, words, and actions to glorify God.
- Husband and wife are not to compete with each other; they are to complete each other in their marriage. The husband is to be the head of the wife (especially as the spiritual leader); the wife is to be his helper.

C. We Should Avoid – Sexual Sin

Genesis 39:9 "No one is greater in this house than I am. My master has withheld nothing from me except you, because you are his wife. How then could I do such a wicked thing and sin against God?"

1 Cor. 6:18 Flee from sexual immorality. All other sins a man commits are outside his body, but he who sins sexually sins against his own body.

Ephesians 5:3-4 But among you there must not be even a hint of sexual immorality, or of any kind of impurity, or of greed, because these are improper for God's holy people. ⁴Nor should there be obscenity, foolish talk or coarse joking, which are out of place, but rather thanksgiving.

Matthew 5:28 "But I tell you that anyone who looks at a woman lustfully has already committed adultery with her in his heart."

Ephesians 5:12 For it is shameful even to mention what the disobedient do in secret.

SO GOD'S WORD TEACHES:

Christian sexual conduct is not based on the agreement of two "consenting adults," but on God's will for the use of this powerful gift. Degrading God's gift of sex by means of jokes, private thoughts, or outward actions displeases God and hurts us.

D. We Should Avoid – Divorce

Matthew 19:6 "So they are no longer two, but one. Therefore what God has joined together, let man not separate."

Matthew 19:9 "I tell you that anyone who divorces his wife, except for marital unfaithfulness, and marries another woman commits adultery."

1 Cor. 7:15 But if the unbeliever leaves, let him do so. A believing man or woman is not bound in such circumstances; God has called us to live in peace.

SO GOD'S WORD TEACHES:
God intends marriage to be life-long. When adultery or malicious desertion takes place, the "innocent" person may get a divorce. God does not, however, approve of "successive polygamy."

FOOD FOR FURTHER THOUGHT

1. What are the responsibilities of Christian parents?

2. What about "children's rights?"

3. Why should a Christian obey a tough, nasty boss at work?

4 When does a person finish his/her responsibility to honor his/her parents?

5. True or False? – "Hatred is not as bad as murder." – Discuss your answer.

6. True or False? – Since the law allows abortions, Christians may get an abortion with a clear conscience.

7. True or False? – It is possible to reach out in love to help an enemy even while he is your enemy.

8. True or False? – Suicide and "mercy-killing" are "open" questions. Each person may decide for himself whether it is right or wrong.

9. Explain why sexual intercourse in marriage is such a blessing.

10. What should a Christian couple do when they are having marital problems?

11. What advice/training would you give a young person looking toward marriage?

12. Give some specific, helpful ways to fight sexual sin.

13. How should Christians view homosexuality? Read **Leviticus 20:13, Romans 1:26**

DAILY GROWTH TROUGH BIBLE READING

1st Day – 1 Corinthians 10
2nd Day – 1 Corinthians 11
3rd Day – 1 Corinthians 12
4th Day – 1 Corinthians 13
5th Day – 1 Corinthians 14
6th Day – 1 Corinthians 15
7th Day – 1 Corinthians 16

A SCRIPTURAL GEM – For the Memory:

Philippians 4:8

Finally, brothers,
whatever is true,
whatever is noble,
whatever is right,
whatever is pure,
whatever is lovely,
whatever is admirable

– if anything is excellent or praiseworthy –
think about such things.

Chapter 12

Love That Directs Life – Toward Others
† 7th – 10th Commandments †

There are many opportunities for God's love to shine through us and our lives toward others. We need the Holy Spirit lest these opportunities are lost.

I. **THE SEVENTH COMMANDMENT: Exodus 20:15** "**You shall not steal.**"
  A. **We Should Be Aware of God's Care**
  Psalm 24:1   The earth is the LORD's, and everything in it, the world, and all who live in it.
  Haggai 2:8   "The silver is mine and the gold is mine," declares the LORD Almighty.
  Psalm 139:14   I praise you because I am fearfully and wonderfully made; your works are wonderful, I know that full well.
  1 Cor. 6:19-20   You are not your own; ^{20}you were bought at a price.

SO GOD'S WORD TEACHES:
  God has wonderfully made us and given us a multitude of material gifts in this life. We should acknowledge His ownership and providence of all we have and are.

  B. **We Should Be Good Stewards (Managers)**
  Romans 14:12   So then, each of us will give an account of himself to God.
  1 Cor. 4:2   Now it is required that those who have been given a trust must prove faithful.

1 Cor. 6:20 Therefore honor God with your bodies.

1 Cor. 16:2 On the first day of every week, each one of you should set aside a sum of money in keeping with his income, saving it up, so that when I come no collections will have to be made.

Eph. 5:16 Making the most of every opportunity, because the days are evil.

1 Peter 4:10 Each one should use whatever gift he has received to serve others, faithfully administering God's grace in its various forms.

Proverbs 19:17 He who is kind to the poor lends to the LORD, and he will reward him for what he has done.

Hebrews 13:16 Do not forget to do good and to share with others, for with such sacrifices God is pleased.

Eph. 4:28 Anyone who has been stealing must steal no longer, but must work, doing something useful with their own hands, that they may have something to share with those in need.

SO GOD'S WORD TEACHES:

- God has given us the privilege and responsibility to manage the gifts He's given us on earth. This is called "Christian stewardship."
- We are accountable for the use of all our gifts – body, time, special abilities, and money.
- Some of our earthly gifts should be used directly in the work of God's kingdom through the Church on earth.
- While the Old Testament required a minimum financial gift of a tithe (10%), New Testament Christians are to give – out of love, regularly, the first of their pay, as God has prospered them. Such percentage-giving God will bless!

- The rest of my material blessings I use to support the Lord's work and share His love with my family, friends, and the poor of this world.

C. We Should Avoid

Eph. 4:28 He who has been stealing must steal no longer, but must work, doing something useful with his own hands, that he may have something to share with those in need.

Lev. 19:35 Do not use dishonest standards when measuring length, weight or quantity.

Jer. 22:13 Woe to him who builds his palace by unrighteousness, his upper rooms by injustice, making his countrymen work for nothing, not paying them for their labor.

2 Thess. 3:10 If a man will not work, he shall not eat.

Psalm 37:21 The wicked borrow and do not repay.

Mal. 3:8 "Will a mere mortal rob God? Yet you rob me. But you ask, 'How are we robbing you?' In tithes and offerings."

SO GOD'S WORD TEACHES:

Any method of taking what rightfully belongs to my neighbor is sinful. That includes robbery, dishonest business practices, unfair wages, laziness, greed, legal technicalities, fraud, and income-tax cheating.

II. THE EIGHTH COMMANDMENT: Exodus 20:16 "You shall not give false testimony against your neighbor."

A. We Should Build Positive Reputations

Proverbs 31:8-9 Speak up for those who cannot speak for themselves, for the rights of all who are destitute. [9]Speak up and judge fairly; defend the rights of the poor and needy.

1 Cor. 13:7 It (love) always protects, always trusts, always hopes, always preserves.

Eph. 4:29 Do not let any unwholesome talk come out of your mouth, but only what is helpful for building others up according to their needs, that it may benefit those who listen.

Eph. 4:25 Therefore each of you must put off falsehood and speak truthfully to his neighbor, for we are all members of one body.

Matthew 18:15 "If your brother sins against you, go and show him his fault, just between the two of you. If he listens to you, you have won your brother over."

SO GOD'S WORD TEACHES:

Our reputation is one of our more prized possessions. Our daily conversation ought to be Christ-like and helpful to those God has placed around us. Our words should encourage and build up God's people to be and live as His people in every way. Personal wrongs should be honestly, personally confronted.

B. We Should Avoid

Proverbs 19:5 A false witness will not go unpunished, and he who pours out lies will not go free.

James 4:11 Brothers, do not slander one another.

Luke 6:37 "Do not judge, and you will not be judged. Do not condemn, and you will not be condemned."

Zech. 8:17 Do not plot evil against your neighbor.

SO GOD'S WORD TEACHES:

False witness, half-truths, slander, gossip, pre-judging, and unkind words are out of place in the Christian's conversation. Unloving words can hurt and cripple as surely as unloving deeds.

***III.* THE NINTH AND TENTH COMMANDMENTS: Exodus 20:17** "You shall not covet your neighbor's house. You shall not covet your neighbor's wife, or his male or female servant, his ox or donkey, or anything that belongs to your neighbor."

   A. **We Should Practice Contentment**

      Hebrews 13:5 Keep your lives free from the love of money and be content with what you have, because God has said, "Never will I leave you; never will I forsake you."

      1 Timothy 6:8 If we have food and clothing, we will be content with that.

      Galatians 5:13 Serve one another in love.

      Psalm 37:4 Take delight in the LORD, and he will give you the desires of your heart.

      Matthew 5:48 "Be perfect, therefore, as your heavenly Father is perfect."

SO GOD'S WORD TEACHES:
As God's children, we should trust Him to provide our needs, and therefore be content with what He provides. We want to please Him in our thinking and desiring as well as in our actions.

   B. **We Should Avoid**

      1 Timothy 6:9-10 Those who want to get rich fall into temptation and a trap and into many foolish and harmful desires that plunge people into ruin and destruction. ¹⁰For the love of money is a root of all kinds of evil. Some people, eager for money, have wandered from the faith and pierced themselves with many griefs.

Isaiah 5:8 Woe to you who add house to house and join field to field till no space is left and you live alone in the land.

James 1:14-15 but each person is tempted when they are dragged away by their own evil desire and enticed. [15]Then, after desire has conceived, it gives birth to sin; and sin, when it is full-grown, gives birth to death.

SO GOD'S WORD TEACHES:

Coveting, as used in these Commandments, is the sinful desire for that which is not yours. We should recognize that sin begins within the heart. Harboring evil desires is sinful.

FOOD FOR FURTHER THOUGHT

1. How should Christians "get involved" with the poor and disadvantaged people around them?

2. What connection does Christian stewardship have with making a will?

3. Is gambling wrong?

4. Many people are on "welfare." – How should Christians treat them?

5. Why is gossip so common, even among Christians?

6. What can you personally do to avoid gossip – for yourself and by others?

7. Why does God expect us Christians to speak up for those being slandered?

Love That Directs Life – Toward Others
† 7ᵗʰ – 10ᵗʰ Commandments †

8. What does "putting the best construction on everything" mean?

9. Is it a sin to be tempted? – Explain.

10. Are all desires for other things wrong?

11. Why is coveting such a deadly sin?

DAILY GROWTH TROUGH BIBLE READING

1ˢᵗ Day – Ephesians 1
2ⁿᵈ Day – Ephesians 2
3ʳᵈ Day – Ephesians 3
4ᵗʰ Day – Ephesians 4
5ᵗʰ Day – Ephesians 5
6ᵗʰ Day – Ephesians 6
7ᵗʰ Day – Philippians 1

A SCRIPTURAL GEM – For the Memory:

Hebrews 13:5
Keep your lives free from the love of money
and be content with what you have,
because God has said,
"Never will I leave you;
never will I forsake you."

Chapter 13

Love That Lasts Forever – the End Times

For many people, love is something you grab while you can, because you can't expect it often and you can't expect it to last.

How different is the love of God given us in Jesus Christ!

– **1 Cor. 13:8** Love never fails. –

Christians confidently look toward eternity.

I. DEATH
A. Definition
Eccles. 12:7 The dust returns to the ground it came from, and the spirit returns to God who gave it.
2 Cor. 5:8 We are confident, I say, and would prefer to be away from the body and at home with the Lord.

SO GOD'S WORD TEACHES:
Death is a separation of the person from his body, the "house" wherein he lives on earth. Scripture gives no directions for caring for the body after death.

B. Soul's Destiny
1. Judgment
Hebrews 9:27 Just as man is destined to die once, and after that to face judgment,

2. **Hell**
   Luke 16:22-23 "The rich man also died and was buried. ²³In hell, where he was in torment…"

3. **Heaven**
   Phil. 1:23 I desire to depart and be with Christ, which is better by far.
   Luke 23:43 Jesus answered him, "I tell you the truth, today you will be with me in paradise." (Spoken to the thief dying on the cross next to Him.)
   Rev. 14:13 "Write this: Blessed are the dead who die in the Lord from now on."
   2 Cor. 5:8 We are confident, I say, and would prefer to be away from the body and at home with the Lord.

SO GOD'S WORD TEACHES:

Life continues after death – either with the Lord in heaven, or separated from Him in hell. Death is but a transition of the soul to one of these places. When a Christian dies, there is – in the midst of sorrow of separation from loved ones – joy that he/she is forever with the Lord.

II. CHRIST COMES AGAIN
A. The Fact
Acts 1:11 "Men of Galilee," they said, "why do you stand here looking into the sky? This same Jesus, who has been taken from you into heaven, will come back to you in the same way you have seen him go into heaven."
2 Peter 3:10 But the day of the Lord will come like a thief. The heavens will disappear with a roar; the

elements will be destroyed by fire, and the earth and everything done in it will be laid bare.

SO GOD'S WORD TEACHES:
It is true. Jesus is coming to earth again!

B. Signs Precede His Return
Read Matthew 24
Wars, rumors of wars, famines, earthquakes, persecution of Christians, false prophets, a falling away from God, wickedness, the Gospel being told all over the world – are all signs of Christ's return.

SO GOD'S WORD TEACHES:
God gave us many specific signs to signal the nearness of the end of the world and the second coming of His Son.

C. The Timing
Acts 17:31 He has set a day when he will judge the world with justice by the man he has appointed.
Mark 13:32 "No one knows about that day or hour, not even the angels in heaven, nor the Son, but only the Father."
2 Peter 3:10 The day of the Lord will come like a thief.
Matthew 24:27 "For as the lightning comes from the east and flashes to the west, so will be the coming of the Son of Man."
1 Peter 4:7 The end of all things is near.

SO GOD'S WORD TEACHES:
Our Lord's second coming will be sudden, unannounced, and unexpected by most people. Scripture knows nothing of a 1000 year rule of Christ on earth before the judgment.

Love That Lasts Forever – the End Times

III. THE RESURRECTION OF THE DEAD

Rev. 1:7 "Look, he is coming with the clouds," and "every eye will see him, even those who pierced him"

2 Cor. 5:10 For we must all appear before the judgment seat of Christ.

John 5:28 "A time is coming when all who are in their graves will hear his voice and come out."

John 11:23-26 Jesus said to her, **"Your brother will rise again."** ²⁴Martha answered, "I know he will rise again in the resurrection at the last day." ²⁵Jesus said to her, **"I am the resurrection and the life. The one who believes in me will live, even though they die; ²⁶and whoever lives by believing in me will never die."**

Job 19:25-27 I know that my redeemer lives, and that in the end he will stand on the earth. ²⁶And after my skin has been destroyed, yet in my flesh I will see God; ²⁷I myself will see him with my own eyes – I, and not another.

SO GOD'S WORD TEACHES:

All who have died over the years will have their souls reunited with their bodies, and will live forever united in body and soul.

IV. JUDGMENT

A. Christ Will Be the Judge

Matthew 25:31 **"When the Son of Man comes in his glory, and all the angels with him, he will sit on his glorious throne."**

Acts 10:42 He commanded us to preach to the people and to testify that he is the one whom God appointed as the judge of the living and the dead.

Acts 17:31 For he has set a day when he will judge the world with justice by the man he has appointed.

2 Cor. 5:10 For we must all appear before the judgment seat of Christ.

SO GOD'S WORD TEACHES:
Jesus will come for the purpose of judging all men in body and soul, and for publicly announcing their eternal destiny.

B. Hell

Matthew 25:41-46 "Then he will say to those on his left, 'Depart from me, you who are cursed, into the eternal fire prepared for the devil and his angels. ⁴²For I was hungry and you gave me nothing to eat, I was thirsty and you gave me nothing to drink, ⁴³I was a stranger and you did not invite me in, I needed clothes and you did not clothe me, I was sick and in prison and you did not look after me.' ⁴⁴They also will answer, 'Lord, when did we see you hungry or thirsty or a stranger or needing clothes or sick or in prison, and did not help you?' ⁴⁵He will reply, 'I tell you the truth, whatever you did not do for one of the least of these, you did not do for me.' ⁴⁶Then they will go away to eternal punishment, but the righteous to eternal life."

John 5:29 "Those who have done evil will rise to be condemned."

Luke 16:22-23 "The rich man also died and was buried. ²³In hell, where he was in torment…"

2 Thess. 1:7-9 This will happen when the Lord Jesus is revealed from heaven in blazing fire with his powerful angels. ⁸He will punish those who do not know God and do not obey the gospel of our Lord Jesus. ⁹They will be punished with everlasting destruction and shut out from the presence of the Lord and from the majesty of his power.

Isaiah 66:24 "the worms that eat them will not die, the fire that burns them will not be quenched, and they will be loathsome to all mankind."

Matthew 10:28 "Do not be afraid of those who kill the body but cannot kill the soul. Rather, be afraid of the one who can destroy both soul and body in hell."

Luke 12:47-48 "That servant who knows his master's will and does not get ready or does not do what his master wants will be beaten with many blows. ⁴⁸But the one who does not know and does things deserving punishment will be beaten with few blows. For everyone who has been given much, much will be demanded; and from the one who has been entrusted with much, much more will be asked."

Matthew 11:20-24 Then Jesus began to denounce the towns in which most of his miracles had been performed, because they did not repent. ²¹"Woe to you, Chorazin! Woe to you, Bethsaida! For if the miracles that were performed in you had been performed in Tyre and Sidon, they would have repented long ago in sackcloth and ashes. ²²But I tell you, it will be more bearable for Tyre and Sidon on the day of judgment than for you. ²³And you, Capernaum, will you be lifted to the heavens? No, you will go down to Hades. For if the miracles that were performed in you had been performed in Sodom, it would have remained to this day. ²⁴But I tell you that it will be more bearable for Sodom on the day of judgment than for you."

SO GOD'S WORD TEACHES:

All who in their faith and life rejected Jesus will be sentenced to eternal separation from their Lord. They will experience only sorrow, sadness, and pain. Those who had the Gospel and rejected it will have a more severe punishment than others.

C. Heaven

Phil. 3:20-21 Our citizenship is in heaven. And we eagerly await a Savior from there, the Lord Jesus Christ, ^{21}who, by the power that enables him to bring everything under his control, will transform our lowly bodies so that they will be like his glorious body.

1 Cor. 15:51-52 Listen, I tell you a mystery: We will not all sleep, but we will all be changed– ^{52}in a flash, in the twinkling of an eye, at the last trumpet. For the trumpet will sound, the dead will be raised imperishable, and we will be changed.

Matthew 25:34 "Then the King will say to those on his right, 'Come, you who are blessed by my Father; take your inheritance, the kingdom prepared for you since the creation of the world.'"

John 5:29 "Those who have done good will rise to live."

John 17:24 "Father, I want those you have given me to be with me where I am, and to see my glory."

Romans 8:18 I consider that our present sufferings are not worth comparing with the glory that will be revealed in us.

1 Cor. 13:12 Now we see but a poor reflection; then we shall see face to face. Now I know in part; then I shall know fully, even as I am fully known.

1 John 3:2 Dear friends, now we are children of God, and what we will be has not yet been made known. But we know that when he appears, we shall be like him, for we shall see him as he is.

Rev. 21:4 He will wipe every tear from our eyes. There will be no more death or mourning or crying or pain, for the old order of things has passed away.

SO GOD'S WORD TEACHES:
Christians still alive when Christ returns will be transformed. All believers will be ushered into heaven. Heaven is where those who love the Lord will always be with Him, serving Him, enjoying His blessings. We are unable to fully comprehend the blessings of heaven. We know, however, it will be more than a thousand times better than our happiest day on earth. We will ever be free from sorrow and pain; we will have a glorified body – like that of our Savior. With all believers, we will be with our God – our Heavenly Father, Jesus our Savior, and the Holy Spirit – forever!

**God's *Powerful Love* will have brought us to our journey's end –
to live with Him in complete peace and joy forever!**

V. OUR CERTAINTY

John 10:27-28 "My sheep listen to my voice; I know them, and they follow me. ^{28}I give them eternal life, and they shall never perish; no one will snatch them out of my hand."

Rev. 2: 10 "Be faithful, even to the point of death, and I will give you life as your victor's crown."

Phil. 1:6 being confident of this, that he who began a good work in you will carry it on to completion until the day of Christ Jesus.

Romans 8:38-39 For I am convinced that neither death nor life, neither angels nor demons, neither the present nor the future, nor any powers, ^{39}neither height nor depth, nor anything else in all creation, will be able to separate us from the love of God that is in Christ Jesus our Lord.

SO GOD'S WORD TEACHES:
Because it is God who gives and nourishes faith and who – through Christ – has prepared a home in heaven for us, as Christians we should always be sure we are going to heaven! What a joy is still before us! We therefore eagerly await Jesus' second coming!

> *He who testifies to these things says,*
> *"Yes, I am coming soon."*
> *Amen. Come, Lord Jesus.*
> *Rev. 22:20*

FOOD FOR FURTHER THOUGHT

1. Why is the teaching of "purgatory" both wrong and potentially deadly?

2. Is it morally wrong to give one's body to science, or to have it cremated?

3. What makes a Christian funeral different from others?

4. Every few years someone "foretells" the precise time when Jesus will come again. Why is this both foolish and wrong?

5. Many denominations believe in some sort of a "millennium" – that Christ will literally rule on earth for a

thousand years before Judgment Day. Explain the falseness of this belief.

6. Since we don't know of the specific details about what heaven will be like, isn't it a bit odd for us Christians to look forward to it so eagerly?

7. If you die today, why are you sure you are going to heaven?

DAILY GROWTH TROUGH BIBLE READING

1st Day – Philippians 2
2nd Day – Philippians 3
3rd Day – Philippians 4
4th Day – Psalm 1
5th Day – Psalm 46
6th Day – Psalm 23
7th Day – Psalm 103

P.S. Continue to read your Bible daily!
Attend a Bible class each week!

A SCRIPTURAL GEM – For the Memory:

John 10:27-28
"My sheep listen to my voice;
   I know them,
     and they follow me.
        ^{28}I give them eternal life,
          and they shall never perish;
              no one will snatch them out of my hand."

About the Author

Born in Illinois, Rev. Dr. Lloyd Strelow was one of fifteen children. He left home as a freshman in high school to begin studies which helped prepare him to become a pastor. As a pastor, he has served six congregations in Michigan and California. His service to the Church at Large has included writing numerous sermon studies published in synodical and other resources, working with large circuit youth retreats, serving as a Circuit Counselor, working extensively with hymns and songs for worship, speaking at numerous events, and serving as Guest Pastor for the *Wittenberg English Ministry* in 2007 for the 490th Anniversary of the Reformation.

Pastor Strelow currently serves on the pastoral staff of *Prince of Peace Lutheran Church* (LCMS) in Hemet, CA, where one of his primary emphases is to teach the basics of the Christian faith to all who seek to know the Lord.

Pastor Strelow is married to Joyce, an RN who has worked in a wide variety of medical facilities. They have been blessed with two children, three grandchildren, and three great-grandchildren. His hobbies include photography and travel, and he enjoys a good laugh. His primary passion is to share God's powerful love in Jesus Christ with others.